SCHOLASTIC

Comprehension Homework Packets

36 Take-Home Packets That Include Short Passages, Graphic Organizers With Questions, and Practice Tests

JAN MEYER

Editor: Mela Ottaiano
Cover design by Maria Lilja
Interior design by Melinda Belter

Interior photos/illustrations: pages 4, 13, and 22: North Wind Picture Archives; page 7: Courtesy of Independence National Historical Park via SODA; pages 10, 28, 34, and 58: Scholastic Photo Archive; page 16: Mona Mark; pages 19, 25, 31, 46, and 55: Library of Congress; page 37: Bettmann/CORBIS; pages 40 and 49: The Granger Collection, New York; page 43: "The Last Spike: May 10, 1869 Union Pacific Railroad, Promontory Point, Utah" Thomas Hill (1829–1908 American)/Scholastic Photo Archive; page 52: Digital Vision/Getty Images; page 61: Sal Veder/AP Photo; page 64: Dorothe Lange/Library of Congress (LC-DIG-fsa-8b32396); page 67: Corbis; page 70: Montgomery County Sheriff's office/AP Photo via SODA; pages 76, 103, and 106: Margeaux Lucas; pages 79, 85, 91, 97, 100, and 109: David Diaz; Design/iStockphoto; page 88: Teresa Southwell; page 94: Teresa Southwell
"Rosie the Riveter" adapted from *Scholastic Action*, © 2005, Scholastic Inc. Used by permission.

D1451050

ISBN-13: 978-0-439-65094-6
ISBN-10: 0-439-65094-1

1 2 3 4 5 6 7 8 9 10   40   15 14 13 12 11 10 09 08 07

NEW YORK • TORONTO • LONDON • AUCKLAND • SYDNEY **Teaching**
MEXICO CITY • NEW DELHI • HONG KONG • BUENOS AIRES *Resources*

CONTENTS

Many students can read words, but they often need help in developing their ability to understand what they read. This book provides practice in building this important skill, which is so necessary for school success. As students read these passages and then work on the companion reading comprehension exercises, they will learn to read for meaning and will gain experience in:

- Building critical-thinking skills
- Becoming purposeful and thoughtful readers
- Remembering key information and paying attention to detail
- Identifying main ideas
- Recognizing cause-and-effect relationships
- Analyzing personality traits, actions, and motivations
- Making inferences and drawing conclusions
- Recalling sequence of events
- Determining the meanings of words in context

THE PASSAGES

This book is divided into two sections: Nonfiction and Fiction. The nonfiction passages focus on important and memorable events in American history from the sixteenth through the twentieth centuries. This section also includes mini-biographies that highlight men and women known for their outstanding achievements and significant contributions in a wide variety of fields.

The fiction selections are all Greek myths. Greek myths have a special appeal for children. These timeless tales are often filled with magic, adventurous deeds, suspense, and emotion. Their characters—gods and goddesses, kings and queens, vulnerable youths, brave heroes, and horrible monsters—are strong and memorable. They'll also read myths about why we hear echoes, why flowers bloom in the spring, and other natural phenomena.

THE READING COMPREHENSION EXERCISES

Following each passage are two reading comprehension exercises that test understanding and retention of what has been read. Students can complete one or both of these exercises, using recall and by scanning the passage to find or verify their answers.

In the Comprehension Check, multiple choice questions in the bubble test format ask the types of questions found in the reading comprehension sections on most statewide and national standardized tests. Completing these tests will help students gain practice and build confidence in their test-taking skills and strategies. Encourage students to read each question carefully to ensure that they understand what is being asked and to consider each answer before making their choice.

Each of the Comprehension Boosters includes a graphic organizer activity and short answer questions that extend and expand learning. The engaging graphic organizer activities help students create a visual representation based on their reading. They will construct a chronology, write headlines, create illustrations, make a timeline, draw a pictorial map, complete a conflict/resolution chart and a belief/supporting evidence chart, and develop an attention-getting flyer. Included as well are the following:

- Venn diagrams for comparing and contrasting
- Sequencing activities for understanding order of events
- Cause-and-effect maps for focusing on relationships and consequences
- A five W's chart that identifies who, what, when, where, and why
- A story map for identifying key elements

Encourage students to use their own words and ideas in completing these activities and the short-answer questions.

At the end of each Comprehension Booster is an optional creative writing prompt—The Write Stuff—related to the passage that students have just read. Many of these springboards to writing are subjects that will give students opportunities to stretch their imaginations and draw upon their own experiences. Others ask students to interpret a famous quote, write a report based on research on the Internet or in a reference book, create a menu of healthy foods, and list ways that weather can harm or help the environment.

The Lost Colony

In 1584 Sir Walter Raleigh, a favored adviser to Queen Elizabeth I, sent an expedition of explorers to America. He hoped they would find a suitable place where England could establish a colony. The men returned with glowing stories about Roanoke, a small island off the coast of our present-day state of North Carolina. They reported that the Native Americans who lived in the area were welcoming, fish were **abundant**, and the soil was so fruitful that the peas they had planted had grown 14 inches in just ten days.

Encouraged by this enthusiastic account, Raleigh recruited about a hundred men to colonize Roanoke Island. By August 1585 these men had crossed the Atlantic Ocean and were building houses and a fort on the island. At first everything went well, but then problems developed. Food became scarce, the promised British supply ships didn't arrive, and the relationship between the colonists and the Native Americans soured. In June 1586 Sir Francis Drake anchored near the island on his way home from the West Indies. Fed up with life in the New World, the colonists sailed back to England with Drake on his ships.

Unwilling to give up, Raleigh made arrangements for another colonizing attempt. This time he included families. They would be more likely, he reasoned, to develop the colony into a permanent settlement. Raleigh chose John White, a member of the first colony, to be the governor. To all who were willing to join the expedition, he offered 500 acres of land.

In July 1587 about 115 men, women, and children arrived on Roanoke. Included in the group were White's pregnant daughter, Eleanor Dare, and her husband, Ananias. The colonists found that the original settlers' fort had been **razed** and the houses had become overgrown with vines. Under White's direction, the settlement was soon rebuilt. There, on August 18, 1587, Eleanor Dare gave birth to a daughter, Virginia, the first English child born in the "New World." Later that month, White sailed back to England to get needed supplies.

A war between England and Spain prevented White from returning to Roanoke until August 1590. When he finally reached the island, however, he found that all the houses had been removed and the settlement had been abandoned. The only clues to the colonists' whereabouts were the letters CRO carved on one tree and the word CROATOAN carved on another. Croatoan, an island south of Roanoke, was where the Croatoan Indians lived. The next day White tried to sail to this island, but fierce storms and rough seas made landing there impossible. White had no choice but to return to England.

In the years that followed, several attempts were made to find the colonists. None were successful. The fate of the lost colonists remains an unsolved mystery.

1. **In the first paragraph, it says that "fish were <u>abundant</u>." Which of these is the best antonym for *abundant*?**

   ○ **A.** tame   ○ **B.** delicious   ○ **C.** scarce   ○ **D.** huge

2. **Which of these is a problem that developed for the first colonists at Roanoke?**

   ○ **A.** The supplies that were supposed to be sent from England didn't arrive.

   ○ **B.** Their relationship with the Native Americans was no longer friendly.

   ○ **C.** Food became hard to find.

   ○ **D.** all of the above

3. **On whose ships did the first colonists return to England?**

   ○ **A.** Sir Francis Drake's   ○ **B.** Ananias Dare's

   ○ **C.** Sir Walter Raleigh's   ○ **D.** Governor John White's

4. **In paragraph four, it says that the "original settlers' fort had been <u>razed</u>." Which of these is the best synonym for *razed*?**

   ○ **A.** enlarged   ○ **B.** destroyed   ○ **C.** decorated   ○ **D.** cleaned

5. **Virginia Dare is often mentioned in American history books. She is remembered because**

   ○ **A.** she was the daughter of Governor John White.

   ○ **B.** she was the first English woman to live in America.

   ○ **C.** she was the only member of the second colony who was found.

   ○ **D.** she was the first English child born in America.

6. **Why did John White sail back to England in August 1587?**

   ○ **A.** He was fed up with life in America.

   ○ **B.** He couldn't find the colonists.

   ○ **C.** He needed to get supplies for the colony.

   ○ **D.** He had to give a report on the settlement to Sir Walter Raleigh.

7. **Which of these states an OPINION about the second colony on Roanoke Island?**

   ○ **A.** The colonists included women and children.

   ○ **B.** The colonists abandoned the settlement to find a place where there was more food.

   ○ **C.** When they arrived on Roanoke, the colonists had to rebuild the settlement.

   ○ **D.** The colonists were offered 500 acres of land by Sir Walter Raleigh.

8. **The second settlement on Roanoke Island is called the Lost Colony because**

   ○ **A.** no one knows where Roanoke Island is.

   ○ **B.** the colonists got lost on their way to the island.

   ○ **C.** no one knows what happened to the colonists who established this settlement.

   ○ **D.** there is no one living on Roanoke Island now.

1. Complete this timeline for Roanoke Island by briefly describing something that happened there in the years 1585, 1586, 1587, and 1590.

1585	1586	1587	1590

2. What evidence did the explorers provide in their report to show that the land on Roanoke was fruitful?

_____

_____

3. Why did Sir Walter Raleigh think families would be good colonists?

_____

_____

4. Why was John White delayed for so long in returning to the second colony?

_____

_____

5. How do you think White felt when he sailed back to England in 1587?

_____

_____

Why did he feel this way? _____

_____

6. Over the years many historians have speculated on what happened to the colonists of the second settlement on Roanoke Island. What do you think *speculate* means? Take a good guess, then look it up in the dictionary to see if you're right.

My guess: _____

The dictionary definition in my own words: _____

_____

The Write Stuff

What do you think happened to the lost colonists of Roanoke? Why do you think they were never found? Do you think they all left Roanoke at the same time? Why do you think they carved the word CROATOAN on a tree? Use your imagination and write your ideas in your journal or on a separate sheet of paper.

Comprehension Homework Packets © 2007 by Jan Meyer, Scholastic Teaching Resources

Benjamin Franklin

Benjamin Franklin was born on January 17, 1706, in a four-room house on Milk Street in Boston. He was the fifteenth child of his father, Josiah, a maker and seller of soaps and candles. After he had attended school for just two years, 10-year-old Benjamin went to work in his father's shop. In his free time he liked to read, fish, go rowing, and swim. Inventive at an early age, he tried floating in a large pond while holding a stick attached to the string of a kite. On windy days, the kite pulled him quickly and smoothly through the water.

When he was 12, Benjamin became an **apprentice** to his brother James, who was a printer. He signed a contract in which he agreed to work without pay for eight years. In return, James agreed to provide him with a room, food, and training as a printer. Benjamin quickly mastered setting type and operating the heavy wooden printing press. At night after work and very early in the morning, he eagerly read book after book on a wide range of subjects.

In 1721 James started a newspaper called the *New England Courant*. The paper was a single sheet, printed on both sides, which included humorous letters to the editor written by James and his friends. To hide their identities, they signed their letters with **fictitious** names like Ichabod Henroost, Harry Meanwell, and Tabitha Talkative. Benjamin wanted to write for the Courant, too. One night he slipped a letter signed "Silence Dogood" under the door of the print shop. To his joy it was printed. He wrote 13 more of these letters in which he made fun of such things as drunkenness and women's hoop petticoats. By 1723, 17-year-old Benjamin was fed up with serving his brother who was often harsh and critical. Without a word to anyone, he ran off to Philadelphia where he found a room to rent and a paying job with a printer.

Just six years later, Benjamin owned his own print shop and newspaper, *The Pennsylvania Gazette*. Both were soon very successful. In 1733 he launched his *Poor Richard's Almanack*, a yearly publication that included weather predictions, verses, helpful information, and wise sayings. Most of these sayings expressed basic truths ("Lost time is never found again") or were meant to advise ("Be slow to choose a friend, slower in changing"). Before long, his cleverly written almanac was one of the most popular publications in the American colonies.

By the time he was 42, Franklin was a wealthy man. He retired from his printing business, but continued to lead a full and productive life. Fascinated by science, he conducted experiments with electricity. He invented a musical instrument, signed the Declaration of Independence, and persuaded the French to aid America in the Revolutionary War. Still politically active at 81, he helped shape the new nation's Constitution. Printer, writer, scientist, inventor, statesman—this man, who accomplished so much, is one of the most important figures in America's history.

1. **Which of these do you think was most likely one of Benjamin's tasks when he worked in his father's shop?**
   - ○ **A.** setting type
   - ○ **B.** trimming wicks for the candles
   - ○ **C.** selling newspapers to the customers
   - ○ **D.** making and selling kites

2. **An <u>apprentice</u> is someone who**
   - ○ **A.** makes predictions about the weather.
   - ○ **B.** writes humorous letters to the editor.
   - ○ **C.** works for little or no pay in exchange for training in a trade or craft.
   - ○ **D.** experiments with electricity.

3. **What was the name of the newspaper that was owned by James Franklin?**
   - ○ **A.** *Poor Richard's Almanack*
   - ○ **B.** *The Pennsylvania Gazette*
   - ○ **C.** the *New England Courant*
   - ○ **D.** the *Boston News-Letter*

4. **In paragraph three, it says that James and his friends signed their letters to the editor with <u>fictitious</u> names. Which of these is the best synonym for *fictitious*?**
   - ○ **A.** well-known
   - ○ **B.** made-up
   - ○ **C.** important
   - ○ **D.** complicated

5. **Why did Benjamin leave Boston in 1723?**
   - ○ **A.** He wanted more free time to read books.
   - ○ **B.** He wanted to be a scientist.
   - ○ **C.** He had completed the agreed-to period of time as his brother's apprentice.
   - ○ **D.** He was tired of working for his strict brother.

6. **One of the sayings in *Poor Richard's Almanack* was, "The sleeping fox catches no poultry." This saying advises against being**
   - ○ **A.** lazy.
   - ○ **B.** hungry.
   - ○ **C.** cowardly.
   - ○ **D.** greedy.

7. **"Lost _____ is never found again." Which of these words correctly completes this wise saying, which is quoted in this biography?**
   - ○ **A.** patience
   - ○ **B.** courage
   - ○ **C.** confidence
   - ○ **D.** time

8. **Which of these sentences states an OPINION about Benjamin Franklin?**
   - ○ **A.** He invented a musical instrument.
   - ○ **B.** When he was 12, he became an apprentice to his brother James.
   - ○ **C.** After he retired, he led a full and productive life.
   - ○ **D.** He was one of the signers of the Declaration of Independence.

Comprehension Homework Packets © 2007 by Jan Meyer Scholastic Teaching Resources

1. In the chart below, compare and contrast yourself with Benjamin Franklin when he was a boy.

	Benjamin Franklin	Myself
Date of birth		
Free-time interests and activities		
Descriptive adjective (and the reason you chose it)		

2. Josiah Franklin had a good business. Why do you think that people at that time needed so many candles?

_____

_____

3. What information is given in this biography that lets you know that Benjamin was part of a large family?

_____

4. Benjamin attended school for only two years, but by the time he was 17 he was well-informed on a number of subjects. How did he acquire this knowledge?

_____

5. Benjamin used the pen name "Silence Dogood" to hide his identity. Write down a pen name that you would use for yourself.

_____

6. What did Franklin do that helped the colonies in their war against the British?

_____

_____

The Write Stuff

In 1771 Franklin began writing his autobiography. Of his second year of school he wrote, "I acquired fair writing, but I failed in the arithmetic and made no progress in it." In your journal or on a separate sheet of paper, write a paragraph that you would include if you were writing your autobiography.

The Boston Tea Party

In 1763 England celebrated a great victory. It had won its war with France and, under the peace treaty, had gained Canada as well as France's lands east of the Mississippi River. The king of England was **jubilant**, but he faced a serious problem. His country needed money! The war had been long and expensive. In addition, there would now be the cost of keeping British soldiers in America to protect England's expanded territory. With the king's encouragement, Parliament decided to raise money by passing laws that taxed the American colonies.

Colonists were outraged by these laws. They had no representation in Parliament. Why then, they argued, should Parliament have the right to pass tax laws affecting the colonies? To demonstrate their anger, many colonists stopped buying English goods.

The resentment of British rule continued. Many colonists believed that England's actions were taking away their basic rights. In 1773 the relationship between the colonies and England became even worse. In May of that year Parliament passed the Tea Act, a law designed to help the British East India Company gain control of all tea sales in the American colonies. To avoid the tax on tea shipped from England, colonial merchants had been selling tea smuggled in from Holland. Now they would lose business to agents for the East India Company, and the hated tea tax would have to be paid.

In the fall of 1773 seven ships loaded with tea from the East India Company set sail for America. The ships that arrived in New York and Philadelphia were met by protesting colonists who forced them to return to England. In Boston, three tea ships arrived. The colonists were determined to send them back, but Thomas Hutchinson, royal governor of the Massachusetts colony, refused to allow this. "The tea must be unloaded," he declared.

Day after day the ships remained in Boston, tied up at Griffin's Wharf. The colonists wouldn't let the ships be unloaded. The governor wouldn't permit the ships to leave. With no acceptable resolution in sight, a group of colonists held secret meetings and hatched a plan. "If the ships aren't sent back, we'll turn Boston Harbor into a teapot," they whispered.

On the evening of December 16, 1773, a large group of men dressed as Mohawk Indians rushed down to Griffin's Wharf. To further hide their identities, they had smeared soot and red paint on their faces. Split into three groups, they boarded each of the ships. The men then hauled the 342 tea chests onto the decks, broke them open with axes, and dumped all of the tea into the water. The ships were left clean and undamaged. Only their cargo was destroyed.

This daring act of **defiance** helped set off a series of events that eventually resulted in America's independence from England. Just 16 months after this "tea party," the Revolutionary War began.

Comprehension Homework Packets © 2007 by Jan Meyer, Scholastic Teaching Resources

1. **What is the main purpose of the first paragraph of this passage?**
   - ○ **A.** to tell who had won the war between England and France.
   - ○ **B.** to explain why England decided to tax the American colonists.
   - ○ **C.** to tell what lands were gained by England in its peace treaty with France.
   - ○ **D.** to explain why the war between France and England was so expensive.

2. **In the first paragraph, it says that "the king of England was <u>jubilant</u>." Which of these is the best antonym for *jubilant*?**
   - ○ **A.** miserable
   - ○ **B.** comfortable
   - ○ **C.** alarmed
   - ○ **D.** happy

3. **The colonists felt that Parliament's laws that taxed the American colonists were**
   - ○ **A.** complicated.
   - ○ **B.** necessary.
   - ○ **C.** unfair.
   - ○ **D.** old-fashioned.

4. **Why was tea smuggled into the colonies from Holland?**
   - ○ **A.** The British had stopped selling English goods to the colonies.
   - ○ **B.** The colonists thought that the tea from Holland tasted better.
   - ○ **C.** The tea shipped from England was being sent back by angry colonists.
   - ○ **D.** The colonists didn't want to pay taxes on the tea shipped from England.

5. **Based on what you read in this passage, you can conclude that Thomas Hutchinson**
   - ○ **A.** took part in dumping the tea into Boston Harbor.
   - ○ **B.** was a member of the British Parliament.
   - ○ **C.** didn't like to drink tea.
   - ○ **D.** was a supporter of England and its laws.

6. **Why did many of the men who took part in the Boston Tea Party wear Indian blankets over their clothes?**
   - ○ **A.** They wanted to get the Mohawk Indians into trouble.
   - ○ **B.** They wanted to stay warm on that cold December night.
   - ○ **C.** They wanted to help hide their identities by dressing as Mohawk Indians.
   - ○ **D.** They thought it would make them look powerful.

7. **In the last paragraph, the Boston Tea Party is described as a "daring act of <u>defiance</u>." The word *defiance* means**
   - ○ **A.** a violent attack on an enemy.
   - ○ **B.** a resistance or challenge to authority.
   - ○ **C.** a celebration of an important event.
   - ○ **D.** an expedition to a dangerous place.

8. **In what year did the Revolutionary War begin?**
   - ○ **A.** 1775
   - ○ **B.** 1773
   - ○ **C.** 1776
   - ○ **D.** 1763

1. In the boxes below, draw two pictures that illustrate what happened at Boston Harbor on the night of December 16, 1773.

2. "No taxation without representation," was often shouted by angry colonists. What does this phrase mean?

   _____

3. What company did Parliament try to help with the Tea Act of 1773?

   _____

   _____

4. Why do you think that the men who took part in the Boston Tea Party wanted to hide their identities?

   _____

5. On how many ships did the Boston Tea Party take place?

   _____

6. In 1774 Parliament passed a group of harsh laws that punished Boston for its "tea party." Angry colonists called these laws the "Intolerable Acts." What do you think *intolerable* means? Take a good guess, then look it up in the dictionary to see if you're right.

   My guess: _____

   The dictionary definition in my own words: _____

   _____

The Write Stuff

How do you think the men felt after they had dumped all of the tea into Boston Harbor? In your journal or on a separate sheet of paper, write about why you think they felt this way. Then write about a time when you felt the same way.

Comprehension Homework Packets © 2007 by Jan Meyer Scholastic Teaching Resources

Sequoyah

In Washington, D.C., there is a bronze statue of Sequoyah in the U.S. Capitol. This Native American of the Cherokee tribe is honored there for the incredible gift he gave to his people: the ability to read and write in their own language.

Sequoyah was born in the 1770s in Taskigi, a Cherokee village in the present-day state of Tennessee. He didn't go to school, and there were no books to read. But he learned many things by listening to the elders' stories about the history and traditions of his tribe.

As he grew older, Sequoyah spent time developing his talent for crafts. He carved objects out of wood with great skill and created beautiful jewelry from silver. In the early 1800s he opened a blacksmith shop where he repaired farm tools and made things from metals. During this time, white settlers were taking more and more land away from the Cherokees. Sequoyah realized that much of the white men's power over his people came from their ability to read and write. Examining pages in their books, he was fascinated by these thin leaves of paper covered with mysterious markings. Soon he began to dream of making "talking leaves" for the Cherokees by finding a way to put their language into writing.

In 1809 Sequoyah began to work on his writing system. At first he tried making pictures to represent words, but he found that many words could not be drawn. Unwilling to give up, he then decided to create a symbol for each of the thousands of Cherokee words. Month after month he filled pieces of bark with markings. Completely **engrossed** in his project, Sequoyah neglected his family responsibilities and his work as a blacksmith. His wife became angry, and his friends made fun of him for wasting his time. As the piles of bark grew ever higher, he finally realized that no one could memorize so many symbols. He needed a new plan.

Sequoyah began to listen carefully to Cherokee words and study the syllable sounds that made up these words. Many of these sounds, he found, were repeated in other words. He became convinced that by making symbols for these syllable sounds, he would be able to combine them and write every word in his language. It took many years, but in 1821 he finished. He had 86 different symbols in his **syllabary** of sounds.

Word of Sequoyah's writing system spread quickly. It was so easy to learn that, before long, many Cherokees were able to read and write their spoken language. They recorded business agreements, wrote down their stories, and sent letters to friends who lived far away. In 1828 the first Native American newspaper was published with articles printed in Cherokee.

The Cherokee National Council presented Sequoyah with a silver medal in recognition of his outstanding contribution. Sequoyah wore this medal with great pride for the rest of his life.

Comprehension Homework Packets © 2007 by Lee Masor Scholastic Teaching Resources

1. **Sequoyah was born in a Cherokee village in what part of the United States?**
   - ○ **A.** the northwest
   - ○ **B.** the southeast
   - ○ **C.** New England
   - ○ **D.** the southwest

2. **When he was a boy, Sequoyah most likely learned from his elders that**
   - ○ **A.** the tyrannosaurus was a huge meat-eating dinosaur.
   - ○ **B.** there are 206 bones in the human body.
   - ○ **C.** animals should be thanked for giving up their lives to feed people.
   - ○ **D.** Jupiter is the largest planet in our solar system.

3. **Which of these things might Sequoyah have made when he worked as a blacksmith?**
   - ○ **A.** iron horseshoes
   - ○ **B.** beautiful baskets made out of twigs
   - ○ **C.** colorful woven blankets
   - ○ **D.** deerskin moccasins decorated with beads

4. **"Talking leaves" as used in this biography refers to**
   - ○ **A.** the sounds made by Cherokee drums.
   - ○ **B.** the sounds heard in the forests when wind blew through the leaves.
   - ○ **C.** arguments that the Cherokees had with white settlers about ownership of land.
   - ○ **D.** sheets of paper covered with writing.

5. **In paragraph five, it says that Sequoyah became completely engrossed in his work. Which of these is the best synonym for *engrossed*?**
   - ○ **A.** upset
   - ○ **B.** bored
   - ○ **C.** fearful
   - ○ **D.** occupied

6. **Sequoyah developed a syllabary. A *syllabary* is a writing system in which the symbols stand for**
   - ○ **A.** the meanings of words.
   - ○ **B.** the letters used in spelling different words.
   - ○ **C.** the sounds of the syllables in words.
   - ○ **D.** individual consonants and individual vowels.

7. **How many years did it take for Sequoyah to develop a writing system for the Cherokee people?**
   - ○ **A.** 5 years
   - ○ **B.** 12 years
   - ○ **C.** 2 years
   - ○ **D.** 9 years

8. **The title that best expresses the main idea of this biography is**
   - ○ **A.** Life in Taskigi, a Cherokee Village
   - ○ **B.** Sequoyah, a Master Craftsman
   - ○ **C.** A Brave Cherokee Warrior
   - ○ **D.** Sequoyah's Gift to the Cherokees

Comprehension Homework Packets © 2007 by Jan Meyer, Scholastic Teaching Resources

1. Listed in the chart below are three descriptive adjectives. Next to each, write a reason why it is a good adjective to describe Sequoyah.

ADJECTIVE	SUPPORT
artistic	
determined	
admired	

2. In what way were white settlers making life increasingly difficult for the Cherokees?

_____

3. Why did Sequoyah's wife become angry with him? _____

_____

4. Sequoyah tried to make a symbol for each word in the Cherokee language. Why did he eventually give up on this approach?

_____

_____

5. These four English words are divided into syllables: *in-ter-est-ing*, *na-tion-al*, *let-ter*, and *in-vi-ta-tion*. Make up a symbol for each different syllable in these words and write the words below using your symbols.

_____

_____

6. Thanks to Sequoyah's writing system, many Cherokees soon became literate. What do you think *literate* means? Take a good guess, then look it up in the dictionary to see if you're right.

My guess: _____

The dictionary definition in my own words: _____

_____

The Write Stuff

What was it like to live in a Cherokee village when Sequoyah was a boy? Use a reference book or the Internet to learn about the Cherokees' way of life. Then write about what you learned in your journal or on a separate piece of paper.

The Lewis and Clark Expedition

In 1803 the United States purchased France's Louisiana Territory, a vast area between the Mississippi River and the Rocky Mountains. That same year, U.S. President Thomas Jefferson asked Meriwether Lewis to lead an expedition through these little-known lands and on to the Pacific Ocean. He wanted a detailed account of the region's geography, plants, animals, and Native American tribes. He also hoped to locate a continuous water route to the Pacific.

Lewis, his co-captain William Clark, and a crew of over 40 men began their journey into the wilderness on May 14, 1804. Starting near St. Louis, they headed up the Missouri River in two canoes and a large keelboat. Pestered by mosquitoes and ticks, the men traveled up the river, making excursions on land and recording their observations in journals. They ate roasted beaver tail, slept in tents, and often struggled upstream against strong river currents.

On August 3 Lewis and Clark held their first official meeting with Native Americans at Council Bluffs in present-day Nebraska. Sitting down with members of the Missouri and Oto tribes, they gave out presents and told the tribesmen of their **benevolent** "great father" in Washington, D.C., who wanted to be their friend. Moving on through the Great Plains, the group saw huge buffalo herds and had a threatening encounter with the powerful Lakota tribe.

The explorers spent the bitterly cold winter at Fort Mandan, a camp they had built in what is now North Dakota. In early April, when the Missouri River was no longer frozen over, part of the group started back to St. Louis in the keelboat packed with plant, rock, and animal specimens for the President. Included was a live prairie dog. The rest of the group, now in eight canoes, continued west. With them was a young Shoshone woman named Sacagawea.

By June this group had reached the Great Falls of the Missouri, around which they had to lug their canoes and supplies. Menaced by rattlesnakes and grizzly bears, they took nearly a month to make their way. In August they came to the area from which Sacagawea had been stolen when she was a child. Hoping to trade for horses for their journey across the steep Rocky Mountains, the men held a meeting at Camp Fortunate with Cameahwait, a Shoshone chief. When Sacagawea arrived to act as their **interpreter**, she burst into tears. Cameahwait was her long-lost brother.

After an exhausting trip across the Rockies, the explorers rested by the Clearwater River in present-day Idaho. Once again able to travel by boat, they moved swiftly downstream on the Clearwater, sometimes upsetting their canoes in **treacherous** rapids. In mid-October they reached the Columbia River where they were greeted by the Wanapam Indians. One month later, having traveled over 4,000 miles in 18 months, Lewis and Clark and their companions arrived on the coast of the Pacific.

Comprehension Homework Packets © 2007 by Ian Mayer Scholastic Teaching Resources

1. **The eastern and western boundaries of the Louisiana Territory were**
   - ○ **A.** the Missouri River and the Rocky Mountains.
   - ○ **B.** the Rocky Mountains and the Columbia River.
   - ○ **C.** the Mississippi River and the Rocky Mountains.
   - ○ **D.** the Mississippi River and the Great Plains.

2. **In paragraph three, the "great father" is described as <u>benevolent</u>. Which of these is the best synonym for *benevolent*?**
   - ○ **A.** impatient
   - ○ **B.** strict
   - ○ **C.** kind
   - ○ **D.** bashful

3. **Why did the explorers stay at Fort Mandan until early April?**
   - ○ **A.** They were waiting for more supplies to arrive from St. Louis.
   - ○ **B.** They were waiting for Sacagawea to join them.
   - ○ **C.** They were waiting for instructions and directions from Thomas Jefferson.
   - ○ **D.** They were waiting for the ice on the Missouri River to melt.

4. **Sacagawea began to cry when she came into the meeting with Cameahwait because**
   - ○ **A.** she was afraid that he would try to steal her.
   - ○ **B.** she was upset at being the only woman in the meeting.
   - ○ **C.** Cameahwait had refused to trade horses for the explorers' goods.
   - ○ **D.** she realized that Cameahwait was her brother.

5. **Lewis and Clark often needed someone to act as an <u>interpreter</u> when they had meetings and conversations with Native Americans. An *interpreter* is someone who**
   - ○ **A.** entertains with drumming and singing performances.
   - ○ **B.** translates or changes words from one language into another language.
   - ○ **C.** is an expert on plants and animals.
   - ○ **D.** serves drinks and snacks to guests.

6. **According to this passage, with which of these Native American tribes did the explorers have a threatening encounter?**
   - ○ **A.** the Lakota tribe
   - ○ **B.** the Shoshone tribe
   - ○ **C.** the Wanapam tribe
   - ○ **D.** the Oto tribe

7. **In the last paragraph, the rapids in the Clearwater River are described as <u>treacherous</u>. Which of these is the best antonym for *treacherous*?**
   - ○ **A.** safe
   - ○ **B.** warm
   - ○ **C.** rough
   - ○ **D.** muddy

8. **Based on what you read in this passage, which of these statements is NOT true?**
   - ○ **A.** The keelboat was sent back to St. Louis from Fort Mandan.
   - ○ **B.** The expedition reached the coast of the Pacific Ocean in mid-November 1805.
   - ○ **C.** The explorers traveled on a continuous water route from the Missouri River to the Pacific.
   - ○ **D.** It took the explorers nearly a month to travel around the Great Falls.

1. In the top section of each box, write the name of a place where the explorers stopped or through which they traveled. In the bottom section, write about something they did or saw in that place. Put the included places in east to west order.

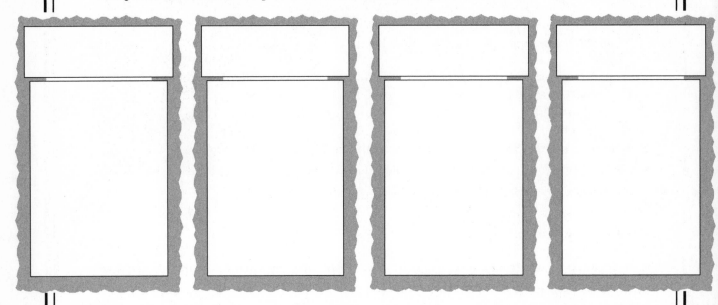

2. What did President Jefferson hope that the Lewis and Clark expedition would locate?

    _____

3. What are three things you think the expedition probably took with them for their journey into the wilderness?

    _____

    _____

4. Lewis and Clark told the Native Americans about their "great father." Who was this "great father"?

    _____

5. What kind of live animal was sent to President Jefferson?

    _____

6. List four discomforts and/or dangers that the explorers faced on their journey west.

    _____

    _____

The Write Stuff

Throughout their journey, Lewis and Clark recorded their experiences and observations in their journals. Now it's your turn! Pick a day coming up soon. At the end of that day, write in your journal or on a separate sheet of paper about the day. Like Lewis and Clark, include detailed descriptions of what you saw, what you did, what you ate, and what the weather was like.

Comprehension Homework Packets © 2007 by Ian Meyer Scholastic Teaching Resources

Sojourner Truth

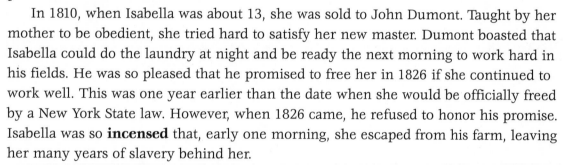

Sojourner Truth was one of our nation's most moving speakers about the evils of slavery. She well understood the suffering and hardships it caused, because she herself had been a slave for nearly 30 years.

Isabella Baumfree (she later renamed herself Sojourner Truth) was born about 1797 in upstate New York. One of her earliest memories was of sleeping crowded together with her parents and her master's other slaves in a damp, unlighted cellar. When she was about 9 years old, Isabella was taken away from her parents and sold to a new owner for $100 and some sheep. One day this new owner beat her so hard that she was left with permanent scars on her back.

In 1810, when Isabella was about 13, she was sold to John Dumont. Taught by her mother to be obedient, she tried hard to satisfy her new master. Dumont boasted that Isabella could do the laundry at night and be ready the next morning to work hard in his fields. He was so pleased that he promised to free her in 1826 if she continued to work well. This was one year earlier than the date when she would be officially freed by a New York State law. However, when 1826 came, he refused to honor his promise. Isabella was so **incensed** that, early one morning, she escaped from his farm, leaving her many years of slavery behind her.

A firm belief in God and the power of prayer gave Isabella strength throughout her life. In 1843 it came to her that she was meant to leave New York City, where she was working as a maid, and spread God's word. She set out with her belongings in a pillowcase and, to mark this new beginning, took the name Sojourner Truth. She chose this name, she explained, because she was going to journey from place to place, preaching truth to the people.

Sojourner traveled around the country for nearly 20 years, speaking out against slavery. During these years she met many of the leaders of the antislavery movement and won their admiration and respect. She also met the women who were leading the fight for women's rights, and she added her powerful voice to this cause as well. Almost six feet tall, Sojourner was an inspiring figure. Her speeches were spirited and stirring and often moved audiences to tears. Never **intimidated** by troublemakers, she faced hooters and hecklers with courage, and she quieted them down with her quick-witted humor and strong words of truth.

In 1863 Abraham Lincoln signed an executive order ending slavery in the rebel states of the South. The following year Sojourner was received by President Lincoln in the White House. Although now close to 70, Sojourner began to work tirelessly to help poor, newly freed slaves try to build better lives for themselves. This brave woman, who devoted so many years to the struggle for freedom and equality, died in 1883.

1. **What evidence is given in this biography that Isabella's second master treated her badly?**

   ○ **A.** He made her sleep in a damp cellar.

   ○ **B.** He made her do laundry at night.

   ○ **C.** He gave her a beating that left scars on her back.

   ○ **D.** He broke a promise that he had made to her.

2. **Why did Isabella work hard for John Dumont?**

   ○ **A.** He treated her very kindly.

   ○ **B.** She liked to work in his fields.

   ○ **C.** He had threatened to beat her if she didn't work well.

   ○ **D.** She had been taught by her mother to be obedient.

3. **In paragraph three, it says that Isabella was so <u>incensed</u> that she ran away from John Dumont's farm. Which of these is the best synonym for *incensed*?**

   ○ **A.** ashamed   ○ **B.** angry   ○ **C.** pleased   ○ **D.** excited

4. **Isabella picked Sojourner as her first name because a sojourner is someone who**

   ○ **A.** had once been a slave.

   ○ **B.** is making a new beginning in his or her life.

   ○ **C.** travels to a place for a short time and then moves on.

   ○ **D.** is very strong and tall.

5. **In paragraph five, it says that Sojourner was "never <u>intimidated</u> by troublemakers." Which of these is the best synonym for *intimidated*?**

   ○ **A.** frightened   ○ **B.** praised   ○ **C.** saddened   ○ **D.** confused

6. **Why was Sojourner able to speak so convincingly about the cruelties of slavery?**

   ○ **A.** She had grown up in the South where slavery was permitted.

   ○ **B.** She had experienced these cruelties when she herself was a slave.

   ○ **C.** She met many slaves as she traveled around the country.

   ○ **D.** She had studied about slavery when she was in school.

7. **Which of these did Sojourner use to help quiet hooters and hecklers?**

   ○ **A.** threats   ○ **B.** tears   ○ **C.** humor   ○ **D.** flattery

8. **Which of these important events happened in 1863?**

   ○ **A.** Sojourner had a meeting with Abraham Lincoln in the White House.

   ○ **B.** Sojourner left New York City to spread God's word.

   ○ **C.** Sojourner died at the age of about 86.

   ○ **D.** Lincoln signed an executive order ending slavery in the rebel states of the South.

1. Cause-and-effect relationships explain why actions and events happen and why decisions are made. In each row below, fill in the missing cause (reason why) or effect (what happened or resulted).

CAUSE	EFFECT
	Isabella was separated from her parents.
	Isabella ran away from John Dumont's farm.
Isabella realized that she was meant to leave New York City and spread God's word.	

2. In which state was Isabella a slave?

_____

3. What two adjectives are used to describe Sojourner's speeches?

_____

4. Sojourner spoke out against slavery. For what other important cause did she speak?

_____

_____

5. Why do you think that Sojourner was admired and respected by leaders of the antislavery movement?

_____

_____

6. What are a few of the problems that you think newly freed slaves might have had?

_____

_____

The Write Stuff

Meeting Abraham Lincoln was a highlight in Sojourner's life. If you could meet a well-known person, who would it be? In your journal or on a separate sheet of paper, write about an imagined meeting with this person. Be sure to include why you would like to meet him or her and what you would talk about.

The Burning of the White House

John Adams, the second President of the United States, was the first President to live in the White House. In November 1800, just four months before the end of his presidency, he and his wife, Abigail, moved into the drafty, unfinished mansion. Only six of the 36 rooms were usable, the grounds were littered with construction equipment, and water had to be carried in buckets from nearly a half mile away.

In 1809, when James Madison became President, the White House still needed considerable attention. The mansion was now more comfortable to live in, but its rooms looked shabby and bare. Madison's wife Dolley and the architect Benjamin Latrobe began a flurry of decorating, using funds approved by Congress. Rooms were repainted or wallpapered, upholstered furniture was purchased, and fancy mirrors were hung on the walls. Dolley ordered a piano she particularly wanted and, over the strong objections of Latrobe, selected red velvet curtains for the drawing room.

Before long the White House looked beautiful, and its public rooms sparkled with frequent teas, parties, and formal dinners. Dolley, a **vivacious** First Lady, became known for her weekly receptions called "Wednesday drawing rooms."

These festive White House events ended in August 1814. Two years earlier, the United States had entered into a war with England over America's rights on the high seas. Fighting had been mainly in the area of the Great Lakes, at sea, and in Canada. Now, however, British forces had sailed into Chesapeake Bay and were headed toward Washington, D.C.

On August 24 Dolley Madison was busy filling trunks with official papers, silver, and her favorite red velvet curtains. Her husband, who was at a nearby battle, had urged her to be ready to flee the White House at a moment's warning. Sure that her husband and his cabinet would soon return, she asked a servant to prepare dinner. At about three o'clock a messenger arrived crying, "Clear out! Clear out!" Dolley refused to leave until a full-length portrait of George Washington was removed from the wall and taken away for safe keeping. At last, leaving behind everything else, she had the trunks put into a wagon and rode away in her carriage.

That night British soldiers broke into the White House. They **gleefully** ate the meal that had been set out, drank President Madison's wines, and grabbed a few souvenirs. Then, using flaming torches, they set fire to the mansion. By the next morning, all that was left of the house were the blackened outer stone walls.

Reconstruction of the White House began in early 1815 under the direction of James Hoban. It took nearly three years for this beautiful mansion to once again be completed.

1. **"Shiver, shiver," wrote Abigail Adams in a letter to her daughter about living in the White House. She most likely used these words because she was**
   - ○ **A.** frightened that the British forces would soon be in Washington, D.C.
   - ○ **B.** excited about just becoming the nation's first lady.
   - ○ **C.** chilly in the cold, drafty mansion.
   - ○ **D.** nervous about living alone in such a large house.

2. **The phrase "Wednesday drawing rooms" refers to**
   - ○ **A.** the rooms in which the Madisons displayed important paintings.
   - ○ **B.** the weekly drawing lessons that were given under the direction of James Hoban.
   - ○ **C.** the rooms in which James Madison and his cabinet drew up and signed official papers.
   - ○ **D.** the receptions that Dolley Madison gave each week in the White House.

3. **In the third paragraph, Dolley Madison is described as <u>vivacious</u>. Which of these is the best synonym for *vivacious*?**
   - ○ **A.** serious
   - ○ **B.** quarrelsome
   - ○ **C.** shy
   - ○ **D.** lively

4. **Why did Dolley Madison ask a servant to prepare dinner on August 24, 1814?**
   - ○ **A.** She wanted to leave something for the British soldiers to eat.
   - ○ **B.** She was giving one of her popular weekly receptions that evening.
   - ○ **C.** She wanted to have a meal ready for her husband and his cabinet when they returned.
   - ○ **D.** She was very hungry after a busy morning of packing.

5. **According to the passage, which of these actions happened first?**
   - ○ **A.** A painting of George Washington was taken away from the mansion for safe keeping.
   - ○ **B.** James Madison left the White House to go to a nearby battle.
   - ○ **C.** A messenger arrived at the White House urging Dolley Madison to leave.
   - ○ **D.** Dolley Madison had the trunks she had packed put into a wagon.

6. **In paragraph six, the British soldiers are described as <u>gleeful</u>. Which of these is the best synonym for *gleeful*?**
   - ○ **A.** cautious
   - ○ **B.** joyful
   - ○ **C.** embarrassed
   - ○ **D.** respectful

7. **In what year did the rebuilding of the White House begin?**
   - ○ **A.** 1815
   - ○ **B.** 1800
   - ○ **C.** 1818
   - ○ **D.** 1810

8. **Based on what you read in this passage, you can conclude that**
   - ○ **A.** Dolley Madison shouted at the British soldiers for drinking her husband's wines.
   - ○ **B.** Benjamin Latrobe thought the red velvet curtains selected by Dolley were beautiful.
   - ○ **C.** the United States won its war with England in 1813.
   - ○ **D.** there was no indoor running water in the White House in 1800.

1. Pictures on storyboards are often used to plan a movie. In the storyboard boxes below, draw three scenes you would show if you were making a movie of the events at the White House on August 24, 1814.

2. The White House now has 132 rooms. How many rooms did it have in 1800?

   _____

3. What musical instrument did Dolley order for the White House?

   _____

4. In 1812 and 1813, where did most of the battles between the American and British take place?

   _____

5. What adjective do you think best describes how Dolley felt as she packed trunks in the White House?

   _____

   Why do you think she felt this way?

   _____

   _____

6. James Madison's medicine chest was one of the items pilfered from the White House on the night of August 24, 1814. What do you think *pilfer* means? Take a good guess, then look it up in the dictionary to see if you're right.

   My guess: _____

   The dictionary definition in my own words: _____

   _____

The Write Stuff

The room where Dolley Madison once held her weekly Wednesday receptions is now called the Red Room. Use the Internet or a reference book to learn some interesting facts about rooms in the White House today. Then write about what you learned in your journal or on a separate sheet of paper.

Susan B. Anthony

On Election Day in 1872, Susan B. Anthony went to the polls in Rochester, New York, and voted. She wanted to challenge the law that barred women from voting. Several weeks later, deputy U.S. marshal E. J. Keeney came to her house and arrested her. At her trial, Judge Ward Hunt ruled that Anthony was guilty of breaking the voting laws. He fined her $100.

Anthony was born on February 15, 1820, in Massachusetts. In 1826 her father moved his family to Battenville, New York, where he opened a large cotton mill. Anthony, who had a quick mind, attended Battenville's one-room schoolhouse. At this school, the boys sat in the front and the girls sat in the back. When Anthony asked to be taught long division, the teacher refused. Such skills, he believed, weren't important for girls to learn. Anthony's father disagreed. He hired a **competent** teacher and started a school for his children in his house.

When she was 20, Anthony accepted a teaching position in Center Falls, New York, for $2.50 a week. The male teacher she replaced had been making $10 a week. Unusually independent for a woman of her time, she turned down the proposals of marriage she received and continued to support herself by teaching.

Following her father's example, Anthony believed that all slaves should be freed and that the drinking of liquor should be stopped. In 1849 she moved to her parents' home in Rochester and began to devote her time to these two causes—the antislavery and temperance movements. In 1853 she became involved in the women's rights movement as well. Working closely with her friend Elizabeth Cady Stanton, Anthony set out to change a New York state law that gave married men ownership of their wives' earnings and property.

After the Civil War, Anthony focused her efforts on gaining passage of a constitutional amendment that would give voting rights to women. She was convinced that women needed suffrage (the right to vote) if they were to have an influence on social and political issues. In 1868 she started a weekly newspaper called *The Revolution*. The following year she and Stanton founded the National Woman Suffrage Association.

Anthony spent the rest of her life fighting for women's suffrage. She traveled tirelessly around the country giving lectures, attending conferences, and gathering signatures on petitions. When she presented these petitions to Congress, many of the senators laughed and treated her with **disdain**. Anthony gave her last public speech at a convention in February 1906. She died one month later at the age of 86. Shortly before her death she declared that failure to gain women's suffrage was impossible. She was right. In 1920 the Nineteenth Amendment to the Constitution became law, finally giving women the right to vote.

1. **Based on what you read in this biography, you can conclude that Anthony's father**
   - ○ **A.** had only one child.
   - ○ **B.** supported the rights of people to own slaves.
   - ○ **C.** spent much of his time in bars and taverns drinking liquor.
   - ○ **D.** believed that both boys and girls should have an equal education.

2. **In paragraph two, it says that Anthony's father "hired a <u>competent</u> teacher." Which of these is the best synonym for *competent*?**
   - ○ **A.** inexperienced   ○ **B.** skilled   ○ **C.** impatient   ○ **D.** friendly

3. **The goal of the temperance movement was to**
   - ○ **A.** end slavery in the United States.
   - ○ **B.** gain the vote for women.
   - ○ **C.** stop people from buying and drinking liquor.
   - ○ **D.** gain equal rights for women.

4. **Which of the following statements about Anthony is true?**
   - ○ **A.** She remained single because no one had asked her to be his wife.
   - ○ **B.** She earned $10 a week as a teacher in Center Falls, New York.
   - ○ **C.** Before the Civil War she spent time working for the antislavery movement.
   - ○ **D.** Shortly before her death she declared that gaining women's suffrage would fail.

5. **Judge Ward Hunt ruled that Anthony was guilty because**
   - ○ **A.** she had voted for a woman.
   - ○ **B.** only men were allowed to vote.
   - ○ **C.** she was not old enough to vote.
   - ○ **D.** she had forgotten to register to vote.

6. **Which of these slogans best expresses the main goal of the women's suffrage movement?**
   - ○ **A.** Women should be seen, not heard!
   - ○ **B.** Equal pay for equal work!
   - ○ **C.** It's our right to keep what we earn!
   - ○ **D.** We're citizens! Let us vote!

7. **In paragraph six, it says that many of the senators treated Anthony with <u>disdain</u>. Which of these is the best antonym for *disdain*?**
   - ○ **A.** respect   ○ **B.** confusion   ○ **C.** disgust   ○ **D.** sorrow

8. **In what year did women gain the right to vote?**
   - ○ **A.** 1872   ○ **B.** 1906   ○ **C.** 1920   ○ **D.** 1820

1. At the end of a biography, there is sometimes a listing of important years and events in the life of the person about whom the biography is written. This listing is arranged in order of time and is called a chronology. Complete this chronology for Susan B. Anthony based on what you read in this biography.

SUSAN B. ANTHONY CHRONOLOGY

1820	Born in Massachusetts on February 15

2. What is one way in which boys and girls were not treated equally at Battenville's one-room schoolhouse?

_____

_____

3. Why did Anthony believe that women needed to be able to vote?

_____

_____

4. Who partnered with Anthony in the founding of the National Woman Suffrage Association?

_____

5. Why do you think that many of the senators laughed when Anthony presented the signed petitions to them?

_____

_____

6. What adjective do you think best describes Susan B. Anthony?

_____

Why did you pick this word? _____

The Write Stuff

Anthony said, "Progress makes the woman of today different from her grandmother." In your journal or on a separate sheet of paper, list ten ways in which the lives of girls and women have changed since the 1800s when Anthony lived.

Elizabeth Blackwell

On a spring day in 1847, Elizabeth Blackwell arrived in Philadelphia. She was 26 years old and eager to enroll in one of the city's medical schools. "You're smart and very determined, but I doubt that any of our schools will accept you," advised Dr. Warrington, a family friend. "No woman has ever been admitted to an American medical school."

As he had predicted, Elizabeth was turned down by all of the schools in Philadelphia. Unwilling to give up, she wrote to schools in other cities and towns. Again she received nothing but rejections. At last, Geneva Medical College, a small school in upstate New York, accepted Elizabeth. Not expecting her to come, its students had voted her in as a joke.

The faculty and students were amazed when the small, plainly dressed woman arrived at the college. But Elizabeth soon impressed everyone. In 1849 she graduated at the top of her class and became the first woman in America to become a doctor.

When Blackwell went to New York City to start her medical practice, she had trouble finding anyone willing to rent office space to a woman doctor. Some thought that examining other people's bodies was shameful behavior for a lady. Others suspected that she was a **quack**. Blackwell finally found a satisfactory place to rent, but only a few patients came.

By 1853 Blackwell's practice was growing, but was still very small. She rented a room in a **squalid** slum area of New York and announced that three afternoons a week she would see patients there at no charge. The people who came to her free clinic lived in crowded, unsanitary conditions that led to the spread of diseases. Blackwell soon realized that these were the patients, especially the women and children, who most needed her care. She must find a way, she decided, to open her own hospital where they could be treated.

Blackwell did find a way. With money from private donations and fund raising fairs, she was able to buy and equip a building in a suitable location. On May 12, 1857, her hospital, the New York Infirmary for Women and Children, opened. Patients who were too poor to pay received medical care for free. Those who could pay were charged 4 dollars a week. The hospital was staffed entirely by women. Blackwell was the director. Her younger sister, Emily, who had become a doctor in 1855, performed operations.

In 1868 Elizabeth and Emily Blackwell started the Woman's Medical College of the New York Infirmary. It grew rapidly and was praised for its high standards of training.

With courage and determination, Elizabeth Blackwell helped pave the way for women to attend medical schools and win acceptance and respect as doctors. At the beginning of this **century**, 45 percent of all medical students in America were women.

1. **Elizabeth Blackwell went to Philadelphia to**
   - ○ **A.** start a medical school for women.
   - ○ **B.** begin her medical practice.
   - ○ **C.** open a hospital for women and children.
   - ○ **D.** seek admittance to a medical school.

2. **The students and faculty at Geneva Medical College were amazed when Elizabeth arrived because**
   - ○ **A.** they had thought she would be tall.
   - ○ **B.** they hadn't realized that she was a woman.
   - ○ **C.** they hadn't expected her to come to the school.
   - ○ **D.** they had thought she would be more elegantly dressed.

3. **In paragraph four, it says that some people suspected that Dr. Blackwell was a quack. A *quack* is**
   - ○ **A.** someone who treats animals.
   - ○ **B.** someone who takes advantage of people by pretending to be a doctor.
   - ○ **C.** someone who sells turkeys, chickens, and ducks.
   - ○ **D.** someone who is very smart.

4. **The patients who came to Dr. Blackwell's one-room clinic**
   - ○ **A.** were Dr. Blackwell's first New York City patients.
   - ○ **B.** could not afford to pay for medical care.
   - ○ **C.** had to travel quite far to come to the clinic.
   - ○ **D.** paid $4.00 a week for treatment.

5. **In paragraph five, it says that Dr. Blackwell "rented a room in a squalid slum area of New York." Which of these is the best antonym for *squalid*?**
   - ○ **A.** clean   ○ **B.** noisy   ○ **C.** busy   ○ **D.** gloomy

6. **In what year did the Blackwell sisters start their medical school for women?**
   - ○ **A.** 1857   ○ **B.** 1868   ○ **C.** 1849   ○ **D.** 1855

7. **In the last paragraph, the percentage of American women attending medical school at the beginning of this century is given. A *century* is a period of**
   - ○ **A.** 100 years.   ○ **B.** 10 years.   ○ **C.** 1,000 years.   ○ **D.** 1 year.

8. **Elizabeth Blackwell is best remembered for**
   - ○ **A.** graduating at the top of her class at Geneva Medical College.
   - ○ **B.** having a sister who was also a doctor.
   - ○ **C.** being the first woman in the United States to become a doctor.
   - ○ **D.** being the director of a hospital for women and children.

1. Below is a list of some of the jobs that were available in the mid-1800s. Place those that you think were performed mostly or only by men in the right section of the Venn diagram. Place those that you think were performed mostly or only by women on the left, and those that you think were performed by both men and women in the center.

governess, lawyer, banker, factory worker, school teacher, newspaper publisher, maid, dentist, dressmaker, shop clerk, carriage driver, bakery worker, nurse, judge, factory owner, hired family cook, police officer, laundress, senator, butcher

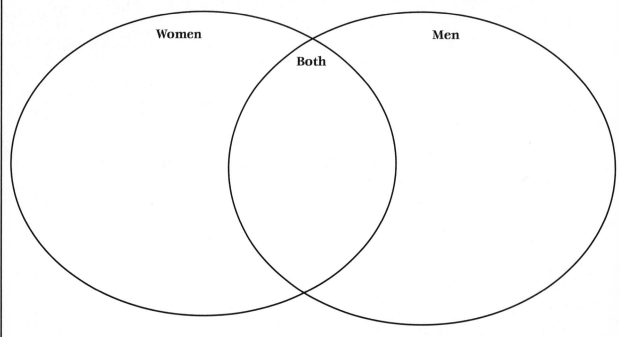

2. Why do you think that many people living in the mid-1800s felt that being a doctor was NOT an appropriate career for women?

_____

_____

3. Why is *courageous* a good word to describe Elizabeth Blackwell?

_____

_____

4. Why were the people who lived in slum areas likely to get sick?

_____

The Write Stuff

Have you ever run into obstacles while trying to do something you wanted to do, go somewhere you wanted to go, or get something you wanted to have? In your journal or on a separate sheet of paper, write about that experience. Be sure to include how you got past or tried to get past the obstacles.

The Underground Railroad

It is said that sometime in 1831 a slave named Tice Davids was being chased by his owner. Davids reached the Ohio River, plunged in, and began to swim for his life. His angry master, who was not far behind, looked around for a boat. Finding one at last, he quickly set off after his slave. Davids, however, vanished from sight when he reached the opposite shore. His owner searched the countryside and the nearby Ohio town but found no trace of his slave. He finally gave up and returned home. "Tice must have gone off on some underground road," he told his friends.

As this story spread, it began to be told that Tice Davids had escaped on an "underground railroad." Soon this became the name for the network of secret routes that slaves followed north to freedom. Before long other railroad terms were used. The houses that hid the slaves became "stations." The owners of the houses became "stationmasters." The **fugitive** slaves were called "passengers," and those who guided slaves to liberty were called "conductors."

Most passengers on the Underground Railroad traveled at night, often using the North Star as their guide. Some rode in farm wagons with false bottoms, but many had to journey on foot. During the day they hid in swamps, forests, or stations in the free states in the North. It took **stamina**, determination, and courage. They were exposed to bad weather and were weakened by hunger. Even worse, they faced the constant risk of being found by professional slave catchers who could even operate in the northern states. That's why many runaways fled all the way to Canada. Once there, they couldn't be captured and returned to slavery.

Both whites and African Americans worked as stationmasters and conductors. Most acted in secrecy because they could be sent to prison or fined for helping slaves escape. The stationmasters hid passengers in attics, root cellars, false closets, and rooms concealed by trap doors. To identify their stations, they often used **prearranged** signals like a quilt hung over a porch railing. Runaways then announced their arrival with a special knock or a password. One of the most active stationmasters was a store owner named Levi Coffin. Known as the "President" of the Underground Railroad, he sheltered about 3,000 slaves over the years.

Conductors had the most dangerous job. They traveled to the South, helped slaves escape, and led them from station to station. Harriet Tubman, an escaped slave, was a fearless conductor. She made 19 trips to the South and guided over 300 passengers to freedom. At one time a reward of $40,000 was offered for her capture.

In 1865, the thirteenth amendment to the Constitution brought an end to slavery. At last the brave efforts of the workers and passengers on the Underground Railroad were no longer needed.

1. **Which of these states an OPINION about Tice Davids?**

   ○ **A.** He swam across the Ohio River.

   ○ **B.** His owner found a boat and set off after him.

   ○ **C.** He went off on an underground road.

   ○ **D.** His owner went home without finding him.

2. **In the second paragraph, it says that _fugitive_ slaves were called "passengers." Which of these is the best synonym for the adjective _fugitive_?**

   ○ **A.** excited   ○ **B.** worried   ○ **C.** disobedient   ○ **D.** fleeing

3. **Why weren't runaway slaves completely safe when they reached the free states in the North?**

   ○ **A.** There weren't any Underground Railroad stations in the North.

   ○ **B.** There were no swamps in which to hide.

   ○ **C.** Almost all northerners were in favor of slavery.

   ○ **D.** They could still be caught there by professional slave catchers.

4. **In paragraph three, it says that escaping slaves needed to have _stamina_. Which of these word pairs are the best synonyms for _stamina_?**

   ○ **A.** politeness and courtesy   ○ **B.** kindness and thoughtfulness

   ○ **C.** strength and endurance   ○ **D.** wisdom and knowledge

5. **Why did most workers on the Underground Railroad operate in secrecy?**

   ○ **A.** They were ashamed to admit that they were helping slaves escape.

   ○ **B.** They could be imprisoned or fined for what they were doing.

   ○ **C.** They didn't want to be rewarded for their efforts.

   ○ **D.** It made it more fun to act in secrecy.

6. **In paragraph four, it says that stationmasters "often used _prearranged_ signals." The word _prearranged_ starts with the prefix _pre_. What is the meaning of this prefix?**

   ○ **A.** not   ○ **B.** before   ○ **C.** after   ○ **D.** many

7. **About how many slaves did Harriet Tubman lead to freedom?**

   ○ **A.** 300   ○ **B.** 19   ○ **C.** 13   ○ **D.** 3,000

8. **Which of these statements about the Underground Railroad is true?**

   ○ **A.** Only white people acted as stationmasters and conductors.

   ○ **B.** Escaping slaves usually traveled during the day.

   ○ **C.** Levi Coffin was an important conductor who guided many slaves north.

   ○ **D.** The final destination for many runaway slaves was Canada.

1. In the chart below, fill in two facts or details for each of these three topics in this passage on the Underground Railroad.

PASSENGERS	CONDUCTORS	STATIONMASTERS
1.	1.	1.
2.	2.	2.

2. Why did Tice Davids' owner think his slave must have taken an underground road?

_____

_____

3. Imagine that you are a stationmaster on the Underground Railroad. What signal would you use to identify your station?

_____

_____

4. "A friend of a friend sent me" was one of the passwords used by slaves when they arrived at a station. Create a password that an arriving slave might use.

_____

5. Why was such a large reward offered for Harriet Tubman's capture?

_____

6. Why do you think Levi Coffin became known as the "President" of the Underground Railroad?

_____

_____

The Write Stuff

When she was a young girl, Harriet Tubman was injured while trying to protect another slave. Use the Internet or a reference book to find out more about this courageous woman. Then write about what you learned in your journal or on a separate sheet of paper.

George Washington Carver

One night in 1864, on a farm in Missouri, a slave named Mary was caring for George, her sick baby. Suddenly slave raiders galloped onto the farm and rode away with them. Moses Carver, the farmer who owned Mary, asked a neighbor to search for her and her son. About a week later the neighbor returned with George, but George's mother was never found.

Moses and his wife Susan raised George as a member of their family. George was not strong enough to assist in the fields, so he helped Susan with her household chores and her garden. Fascinated by plants, he developed a talent for taking care of them. He became so good at nursing sickly plants that he became known in the area as "the plant doctor."

George was eager to go to school, but the nearest school for black children was in Neosho, a town eight miles away. When he was 12, George left the Carvers, taking their last name as his own, and walked to Neosho. After living there for a year, he had learned all that the one-room school could offer. Anxious to learn as much as possible, he moved on. For the next three years, he traveled from town to town, attending schools and finding work. By 1880 he was living in Kansas where he set up a small laundry business and attended high school.

When he was in his mid-20s, Carver enrolled at Iowa State College to study science and pursue a career in agriculture. He completed a master's degree there in 1896. That same year, Carver moved to Alabama. He had been invited to become the head of the new department of agriculture at Tuskegee Institute. His responsibilities included teaching, directing crop and soil experiments, and giving agricultural advice to farmers in outlying areas. Carver was particularly concerned about the **plight** of poor black farmers. To help these farmers, he held conferences and wrote easy-to-read booklets on such topics as inexpensive farming methods and meals to cook for good nutrition. He even designed and equipped a wagon, called the Jesup Wagon, which could be driven to rural areas for demonstrations.

Most of these **impoverished** farmers worked on land that had been worn out by planting cotton year after year. Carver advised them to plant peanuts, a food rich in protein and a crop that would put minerals back into the soil. Many farmers followed his advice, but there was a limited market for their peanuts. Carver realized that he had to increase the demand for this crop. He worked long hours in his laboratory and, in time, developed over 300 products made from peanuts including cooking oil, shaving cream, printer's ink, candy, and soap.

Although Carver's work with peanuts brought him national fame, he remained at Tuskegee, living in two small rooms. He had no interest in acquiring possessions or gaining personal wealth. "These mean nothing," he said. "It is simply service that measures success."

1. **George became known as "the plant doctor" because**
   - ○ **A.** he knew which plants could be used to treat sicknesses.
   - ○ **B.** he liked to wear a white coat when he worked in the garden.
   - ○ **C.** he knew how to make ailing plants become healthy again.
   - ○ **D.** he made medicines out of plants in his laboratory.

2. **Why did George leave the Carvers and move to Neosho?**
   - ○ **A.** He wanted to look for his mother.
   - ○ **B.** He wanted to go to school.
   - ○ **C.** He was tired of helping Mrs. Carver with her household chores.
   - ○ **D.** He wanted to open a laundry.

3. **In paragraph four, it says that "Carver was particularly concerned with the plight of poor black farmers." Which of these is the best synonym for *plight*?**
   - ○ **A.** problems   ○ **B.** rudeness   ○ **C.** shyness   ○ **D.** ambition

4. **What was the Jesup Wagon used for?**
   - ○ **A.** carrying picked cotton from the fields
   - ○ **B.** hauling peanuts to market
   - ○ **C.** taking farmers into town to go shopping
   - ○ **D.** showing farming methods to farmers

5. **In paragraph five, those Carver wanted to help are described as impoverished. Which of these is the best antonym for *impoverished*?**
   - ○ **A.** lonely   ○ **B.** rich   ○ **C.** intelligent   ○ **D.** healthy

6. **What is one of the reasons why Carver encouraged the farmers to grow peanuts?**
   - ○ **A.** There was a limited market for cotton.
   - ○ **B.** Peanuts are a healthy food to eat because they are a good source of protein.
   - ○ **C.** They would be able to make peanut candy.
   - ○ **D.** Growing peanuts would make them famous.

7. **With which of these statements would Carver have agreed?**
   - ○ **A.** A successful person is someone who becomes famous.
   - ○ **B.** A successful person is someone who drives an expensive car.
   - ○ **C.** A successful person is someone who helps to improve the lives of others.
   - ○ **D.** A successful person is someone who makes a lot of money.

8. **What made Carver's accomplishments particularly remarkable?**
   - ○ **A.** He had had very little education.
   - ○ **B.** When he was a child, he was not very strong.
   - ○ **C.** He was a scientist.
   - ○ **D.** He had been born as a slave.

1. Carver had lived in four different places by the time he was 35. In the chart below, list these states in the order in which he lived in them. Then, to the right of each state name, write a sentence about something he did when he was living there.

State	Something He Did There

2. Why did George leave Neosho?

_____

_____

3. What were two of Carver's responsibilities at Tuskegee?

_____

_____

4. Planting cotton year after year had depleted the soil of important minerals. What do you think *deplete* means? Take a good guess, then look it up in the dictionary to see if you're right.

My guess: _____

The dictionary definition in my own words: _____

_____

5. Carver developed over 300 products from peanuts. How did this help the farmers?

_____

_____

The Write Stuff

Carver wanted to help improve the diet of poor black farmers. He even included recipes in his booklets. In your journal or on a separate sheet of paper, create a menu for a healthy lunch or a healthy dinner.

Women of the Civil War

During the Civil War, northern and southern women found their lives greatly changed. Proving they were not as delicate and dependent as many had believed, they took on new roles and challenges. In addition to carrying on the responsibilities of men in their families who had left for the battlefields, large numbers of women took an active part in the war effort.

Eager to help the Union, women throughout the North formed soldiers' aid societies. At gatherings in homes and churches, they made uniforms, knit socks, and packed up donations of food and medicines. In Chicago and other northern cities, women organized fairs that raised thousands of dollars for the war. In the South, women rolled bandages, sewed clothes, and raised money for the Confederate Army. Some took meals and cold drinks to their troops at train stations. Others wrote encouraging letters to all the soldiers they knew.

Many women on both sides of the conflict left their homes to become nurses. Exposed to the horrors of war, these women cleaned bloody wounds, wiped feverish faces, and comforted the dying. Most had little training and worked long hours under difficult conditions. Some, like Mary Ann Bickerdyke (above), worked in field hospitals that were close to the fighting. "Mother" Bickerdyke, as she was called, tenderly cared for injured Union soldiers at 19 different battle sites. At night, she often went to the battlefields to search for wounded men.

Although only males were allowed to enlist, at least 400 women became soldiers by disguising themselves as men. Jennie Hodgers served as a Union soldier for three years using the name Albert Cashier. Fighting with as much **valor** as the men, she faced enemy fire in more than 35 battles. Some women joined the troops looking for excitement and adventure. Others, like Malinda Blalock, wanted to be near their husbands. She enlisted in the Confederate Army posing as her husband's brother Samuel.

A surprising number of women risked punishment by acting as spies. One of the South's most **celebrated** spies was Rose O'Neal Greenhow. A popular hostess in Washington, D.C., she knew many Union government and military leaders. She learned all she could from them and then sent the information in code to Confederate officers. Sarah Edmonds, a spy for the North, was a master of disguises. One time she went to Confederate camps dressed as a peddler. She gathered information from the soldiers as she sold them her goods.

By the end of the Civil War, many women had gained confidence in their abilities and a sense of pride in having taken on new responsibilities. Whether they lived in the North or the South, these women had exhibited determination and courage in helping to support a cause in which they believed.

1. **Which of these was most likely a new responsibility for many wives during the Civil War?**

   ○ **A.** caring for children when they were sick

   ○ **B.** managing the family's money

   ○ **C.** tending a flower garden

   ○ **D.** planning meals for the family

2. **At how many battle sites did "Mother" Bickerdyke nurse wounded soldiers?**

   ○ **A.** more than 35   ○ **B.** 19   ○ **C.** 400   ○ **D.** 3

3. **What is the most likely reason why Mary Ann Bickerdyke was called "Mother" Bickerdyke by the wounded soldiers she tended?**

   ○ **A.** The soldiers knew that she had a large number of children.

   ○ **B.** She insisted that they use good table manners when they ate their meals.

   ○ **C.** Most of these wounded soldiers were her sons.

   ○ **D.** Her comforting care for them was like that of a mother.

4. **Why did Sarah Edmonds go to Confederate camps dressed like a peddler?**

   ○ **A.** She wanted to raise money for the war by selling goods.

   ○ **B.** She was looking for wounded soldiers who needed care.

   ○ **C.** She wanted to help them get needed supplies and clothing.

   ○ **D.** She wanted to learn about the soldiers' war plans.

5. **In paragraph four, it says that Jennie Hodgers fought with <u>valor</u>. Which of these is the best antonym for *valor*?**

   ○ **A.** strength   ○ **B.** affection   ○ **C.** cowardice   ○ **D.** sorrow

6. **Based on what you read in this passage, which of these statements is NOT true?**

   ○ **A.** Rose O'Neal Greenhow sent coded messages to Union military leaders.

   ○ **B.** Only men were allowed to enlist as soldiers.

   ○ **C.** A fair was held in Chicago to raise money for the war.

   ○ **D.** Most Civil War nurses received little training.

7. **Which of these is the best synonym for <u>celebrated</u> as it is used in paragraph five?**

   ○ **A.** entertaining   ○ **B.** famous   ○ **C.** boastful   ○ **D.** generous

8. **The author's main purpose in writing this passage was to**

   ○ **A.** tell about the horrors and hardships of the Civil War.

   ○ **B.** contrast the war activities of northern women with those of southern women.

   ○ **C.** show that women played an important role in the Civil War.

   ○ **D.** explain how differently wars were fought in the 1800s.

1. Listed in the chart below are three adjectives that describe many women who took part in the Civil War effort. Next to each, give an example of how the characteristic was exhibited by a group of women or a specific woman.

ADJECTIVE	EXAMPLE
caring	
brave	
clever	

2. According to the passage, what two words were used by many to describe women in the years before the Civil War?

_____

3. What did the women in soldiers' aid societies do?

_____

_____

4. Why do you think only men could enlist as soldiers in the Civil War?

_____

_____

5. What were two different reasons why some women became soldiers?

_____

_____

6. Both the North and the South used espionage to find out about their enemy's war plans and strategies. What do you think *espionage* means? Take a good guess, then look it up in the dictionary to see if you're right.

My guess: _____

The dictionary definition in my own words: _____

_____

The Write Stuff

A number of women including Rose O'Neal Greenhow and Sarah Edmonds wrote books about their Civil War experiences. In your journal or on a separate sheet of paper, describe in detail an important experience or event in your life. Be sure to include when it happened and how you felt.

Laura Ingalls Wilder

In 1873 6-year-old Laura Ingalls was living in a log cabin in a thickly wooded area of Wisconsin. Called "Little Half-Pint" by her father, she was adventurous and lively. When she wasn't helping her mother with chores, she climbed trees and played ball. After supper, she loved to sit by the fire and listen to her father tell stories and play his fiddle.

When Laura was 7, she and her family headed west in a covered wagon for the open prairies of Minnesota. They settled there on the banks of Plum Creek. Laura walked two miles into town to attend school. At home, she liked to wade in the creek and pick wildflowers that grew among the tall prairie grasses. She helped her father plant wheat, but before it could be harvested, swarms of chomping grasshoppers descended and stripped his fields bare.

By 1880 Laura was living in De Smet, a new town in the Dakota Territory. Laura continued her schooling, earned money as a teacher, and began to take part in the social life of the growing town. She attended ice-cream socials, went on church picnics, and took long rides in a horse-drawn buggy with a young farmer named Almanzo Wilder.

Laura married Almanzo when she was 18. At her wedding she wore a black cashmere dress she had made. The early years of her marriage brought both joy and **misfortune**. In 1886 Laura gave birth to a daughter they named Rose. Two years later, though, their house burned down, their newly born son died, and hot weather dried up their crops. Hoping for better opportunities, the Wilders moved to Florida, back to De Smet, and then to the Ozark Mountains of Missouri. They bought a farm there, using $100 that they had managed to save for the down payment. Laura's years of moving were finally over.

While in her 40s, Laura began adding to their small income by writing articles for the *Missouri Ruralist*, a newspaper for farmers. In time she had her own column that she wrote twice a month through 1925. During these years Laura thought about how much her life had changed. She now took rides with Almanzo in a car they had named Isabel, and her house had a phone, electricity, and a radio. Wanting to keep alive what it had been like to live as a pioneer on the American frontier, she began writing down memories of her childhood.

With her daughter Rose's help, Laura turned what she had written into a children's book titled *Little House in the Big Woods*. It was published in 1932 when Laura was 65. She went on to write six more "Little House" books based on her childhood and teen years. The books received **accolades** from the critics, and thousands of young fans wrote her letters.

Laura Ingalls Wilder's stories about pioneer life live on. Her books are still very popular today and have been translated into a number of languages.

1. **Which of these statements about Laura's childhood is NOT true?**
   - ○ **A.** She liked to spend most of her free time playing quietly indoors.
   - ○ **B.** She had to walk two miles into town to attend school.
   - ○ **C.** She traveled with her family in a covered wagon.
   - ○ **D.** Her father had a special name for her.

2. **The Ingalls left Wisconsin and moved to a home**
   - ○ **A.** in the mountains.
   - ○ **B.** on the open prairie.
   - ○ **C.** in a big woods.
   - ○ **D.** on the shores of a lake.

3. **In paragraph four, it says that "the early years of her marriage brought both joy and misfortune." Which of these is the best antonym for _misfortune_?**
   - ○ **A.** good luck
   - ○ **B.** adventure
   - ○ **C.** ambition
   - ○ **D.** illness

4. **Why was 1886 a memorable year for Laura?**
   - ○ **A.** She got married to Almanzo Wilder.
   - ○ **B.** She published her first book.
   - ○ **C.** She moved for the last time.
   - ○ **D.** She gave birth to a daughter.

5. **Why did the Wilders move to Florida?**
   - ○ **A.** Their wheat crop had been ruined by grasshoppers.
   - ○ **B.** Laura had an opportunity to write for a farm magazine there.
   - ○ **C.** They hoped to find a better life for themselves there.
   - ○ **D.** Laura wanted to live near her parents.

6. **When Laura was in her 40s and 50s, she thought about how much her life had changed. One important change was that**
   - ○ **A.** she no longer lived on a farm.
   - ○ **B.** she was now very rich.
   - ○ **C.** modern conveniences were making her life more comfortable.
   - ○ **D.** she had become a well-known author of books for children.

7. **Based on what you read in Laura's biography, in which of her books do you think she described an invasion of grasshoppers?**
   - ○ **A.** _Little House in the Big Woods_
   - ○ **B.** _On the Banks of Plum Creek_
   - ○ **C.** _By the Shores of Silver Lake_
   - ○ **D.** _The Long Winter_

8. **In paragraph six, it says that Laura's "books received _accolades_ from the critics." Which of these is the best synonym for _accolades_?**
   - ○ **A.** questions
   - ○ **B.** disapproval
   - ○ **C.** praise
   - ○ **D.** suggestions

1. Laura's first book, *Little House in the Big Woods*, is based on her experiences when she and her family lived in Wisconsin. *On the Banks of Plum Creek* is based on her experiences when the Ingalls lived in Minnesota. In the boxes below, create an illustration that would be appropriate for each of these books.

Little House in the Big Woods　　　　　*On the Banks of Plum Creek*

2. What are two things that you can do that a pioneer girl living in the 1870s was not able to do?

_____

_____

3. What evidence is given in this biography that Laura had learned how to make clothing?

_____

4. Why did Laura want to write about her childhood? _____

_____

5. What name did Almanzo and Laura give to their car?

_____

6. What has made it possible for children in countries like Japan and Mexico to read the "Little House" books?

_____

_____

The Write Stuff

Laura had a talent for writing descriptions. In her book *Little House in the Big Woods*, she describes a small store where her father sold furs he had trapped. In your journal or on a separate sheet of paper, write a detailed description of a store that you like to go to.

The Transcontinental Railroad

Abraham Lincoln believed that building a railroad across the undeveloped lands of the West would be of great benefit to the country. In 1862 he signed the Pacific Railroad Act, which provided land and government loans for the construction of a **transcontinental** railroad stretching from California to the Missouri River. The act gave responsibility for building the line to two companies. The Union Pacific was to build westward from Omaha, Nebraska, while the Central Pacific was to build eastward from Sacramento, California.

In 1863 the companies set to work, each one hoping to construct more miles of track than the other. Surveyors began to map the best routes. In time they were followed by graders who prepared and leveled the road beds. As the graders moved forward, other workers laid down tracks, fastening the rails to the wooden ties with spikes. Little progress was made, though. Both companies had trouble finding laborers, and the Civil War caused shortages of materials.

The war ended in April 1865. By the following spring the Union Pacific had hired thousands of former soldiers, a majority of whom were Irish immigrants. Mile after mile, these workers pushed west across the Great Plains. At night they slept in boxcars that contained bunks three tiers high. During the day they worked from sunup to sundown, often braving harsh weather and attacks by Plains Indians who were angered by this **intrusion** on their buffalo hunting grounds.

The Central Pacific solved its labor problems in 1865 by adding thousands of Chinese immigrants to its crew of workers. This workforce, now about 80 percent Chinese, headed east through California's soaring Sierra Nevada Mountains. Using drills and explosives, blasting crews labored underground night and day to make 15 tunnels through the hard granite mountains. It was slow, dangerous work. There were avalanches, many blasting-powder accidents, and winter storms that sometimes dropped over ten feet of snow. Finally, in June 1868, the Central Pacific's road beds and rails through the Sierras were finished. Its track layers could now press forward at full speed across Nevada's flat desert.

By 1869 workers for both the Union Pacific and the Central Pacific were spiking down rails in the Utah Territory. On May 10, 1869, the tracks of these two companies were finally joined in a ceremony at Promontory Point, north of the Great Salt Lake. The Union Pacific had laid 1,086 miles of track. The Central Pacific had laid 690 miles of track. To mark the transcontinental railroad's completion, a gold spike was hammered into the last rail. As word spread that the tracks had been linked, people across the nation celebrated this great feat of engineering, made possible by the **grueling** labor of thousands of tough, brave men.

1. <u>Transcontinental</u> begins with the prefix *trans*. What is the meaning of this prefix?

   ○ **A.** under   ○ **B.** across   ○ **C.** after   ○ **D.** against

2. **Which of these is something a grader for the railroads might have done?**

   ○ **A.** looked for the best place to build a railroad bridge across a stream

   ○ **B.** pounded down spikes with a sledgehammer

   ○ **C.** lifted and set heavy iron rails into place

   ○ **D.** used a pick and a shovel to remove rocks from a road bed

3. **The Union Pacific's progress across the Great Plains was much faster than the Central Pacific's progress through the Sierras. Why do you think that was?**

   ○ **A.** The Irish immigrants were much better workers than the Chinese immigrants.

   ○ **B.** The Union Pacific workers had help from the Plains Indians.

   ○ **C.** It was faster and easier to build a railroad line across flat, open plains.

   ○ **D.** The Central Pacific's work days were much shorter.

4. **What important historical event happened in April 1865?**

   ○ **A.** Abraham Lincoln signed the Pacific Railroad Act.

   ○ **B.** The transcontinental railroad was completed.

   ○ **C.** The Civil War ended.

   ○ **D.** The Central Pacific's rail lines through the Sierras were finished.

5. **In paragraph three, it says that the Plains Indians "were angered by this <u>intrusion</u> on their buffalo hunting grounds." An *intrusion* is**

   ○ **A.** a loud, noisy party

   ○ **B.** an unwanted presence in someone else's space

   ○ **C.** a boxcar that is filled with bunks for sleeping

   ○ **D.** a long, underground tunnel

6. **How long did it take to build the transcontinental railroad?**

   ○ **A.** about six years   ○ **B.** about three years

   ○ **C.** about ten years   ○ **D.** about one year

7. **Which of the following statements about the transcontinental railroad is NOT true?**

   ○ **A.** The Union Pacific solved its labor problems by hiring thousands of former soldiers.

   ○ **B.** Workers for the Central Pacific used explosives to make tunnels through the Sierras.

   ○ **C.** A ceremony was held at Promontory Point to spike down the last rail.

   ○ **D.** The Central Pacific laid more miles of track than the Union Pacific.

8. **In the last paragraph, the workers' labor is described as <u>grueling</u>. Which of these is the best synonym for *grueling*?**

   ○ **A.** careless   ○ **B.** interesting   ○ **C.** patriotic   ○ **D.** exhausting

Comprehension Homework Packets © 2007 by Joe Moore Scholastic Teaching Resources

1. Use this Venn diagram to compare the two railroad companies as described in this passage. On the left and the right, list the differences between their workers, where they worked, the kind of work they did, and the problems and dangers they faced. In the center, list things that were the same for both companies.

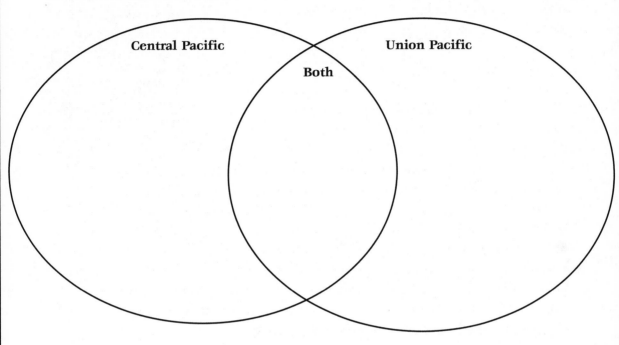

Central Pacific   **Both**   **Union Pacific**

2. How do you think people traveled to California before the transcontinental railroad was built?

_____

_____

3. What was the responsibility of the men who were surveyors for the railroad?

_____

_____

4. Why do you think that *tough* and *brave* are good words to describe the railroad workers?

_____

_____

The Write Stuff

Travel today is much easier than it was in the 1800s. In your journal or on a separate sheet of paper, write about a trip that you've taken. Be sure to include where you went, how you got there, who went with you, and what you did on this trip.

The Wright Brothers

When Wilbur Wright was 11 and his brother Orville was 7, their father gave them a toy helicopter that was powered by a rubber band. They played with it again and again. It was this amazing toy, Orville later recalled, that first sparked their interest in flight.

In 1892 the Wright brothers, now in their 20s, opened a shop in Dayton, Ohio, where they sold, repaired, and built bicycles. Once their business was well established, they began reading everything they could find on flying machines and on the principles of **aeronautics**. They were particularly interested in the experiments of Otto Lilienthal, a German engineer. Called "Flying Man," Lilienthal had made over 2,000 short flights hanging from gliders.

Wilbur and Orville learned that a heavier-than-air flying machine needed three things: wings to lift it into the air, a power source, and a system for controlling it. The biggest problem, still far from being solved, was finding a way to control the machine during flight. In 1899 the brothers came up with an important idea. They observed that birds make turns and balance themselves by changing the position and angle of their outstretched wings. This, they decided, might be the key to successfully maneuvering an aircraft through the air.

To test their idea, the brothers designed a kite with two long, flexible wings. Cords attached to these wings controlled their angles. Encouraged by the kite's performance, they then built a series of full-size gliders. Working tirelessly, they experimented with different wing and tail rudder designs. Finally, in the fall of 1902, the brothers succeeded in piloting a number of controlled glides. Now they were ready to build an airplane with an engine.

On December 17, 1903, the brothers stood alone on a sand dune at Kill Devil Hills, near Kitty Hawk, North Carolina. They had chosen this place for testing their airplane because it had plenty of open space and strong, steady winds. The brothers' airplane, named the *Flyer*, sat nearby. It had cloth-covered wings, two propellers, a lightweight gasoline engine they had built, and controls similar to those in their 1902 glider. Four men arrived to help haul the *Flyer* onto its takeoff rail and to act as witnesses. About to risk injury or even death, Orville lay down on his stomach in the center of the lower wing and started the engine. The *Flyer* moved down the rail, lifted into the air, and flew 120 feet before it thumped down on the sand.

The Wright brothers made three more flights that historic day. On the last and longest flight, Wilbur flew the Flyer a distance of 852 feet and was in the air for 59 seconds. The brothers were **elated**. They had become the first in the world to pilot and control a powered aircraft. As Orville and Wilbur wrote in a press release that they sent out to the newspapers, "The age of the flying machine has come at last."

1. **What or who was called "Flying Man?"**
   - ○ **A.** the toy helicopter that was given to Wilbur and Orville
   - ○ **B.** Otto Lilienthal, the German engineer
   - ○ **C.** the Wright brothers' powered airplane
   - ○ **D.** Orville Wright

2. **When Orville and Wilbur were in their 20s, they opened a shop where they sold, repaired, and built**
   - ○ **A.** toys.　　○ **B.** kites.　　○ **C.** gliders.　　○ **D.** bicycles.

3. **The brothers' idea for a way to control an aircraft in the air was inspired by**
   - ○ **A.** their observations of the flying performance of kites.
   - ○ **B.** the articles and books they read on flying machines.
   - ○ **C.** the experiments of Otto Lilienthal.
   - ○ **D.** their observations of birds in flight.

4. **In paragraph two, it says that the Wright brothers read materials on the principles of <u>aeronautics</u>. The term *aeronautics* refers to the science having to do with**
   - ○ **A.** weather patterns and wind strengths.
   - ○ **B.** the design, manufacture, and flying of aircraft.
   - ○ **C.** the testing and operation of engines.
   - ○ **D.** the balance requirements of bicycles.

5. **What was one of the reasons that the Wright brothers tested their powered airplane at Kill Devil Hills?**
   - ○ **A.** It was warmer in North Carolina than it was in Ohio.
   - ○ **B.** They wanted their airplane to take off from the top of a hill.
   - ○ **C.** It was an area that had a lot of open space.
   - ○ **D.** It had the country's best equipped airport.

6. **Which was the Wright brothers' longest flight on December 17, 1903?**
   - ○ **A.** the fourth flight　　　　　○ **B.** the first flight
   - ○ **C.** the third flight　　　　　○ **D.** the second flight

7. **Based on what you read in this passage, you can conclude that**
   - ○ **A.** very large crowds watched the *Flyer*'s first flight on that December day.
   - ○ **B.** the Wright brothers were also the first to fly in the air on gliders.
   - ○ **C.** only Orville was daring enough to try piloting the *Flyer* on that December day.
   - ○ **D.** Orville and Wilbur were very good mechanics.

8. **In the last paragraph, it says that the Wright brothers were <u>elated</u>. Which of these is the best synonym for *elated*?**
   - ○ **A.** ambitious　　○ **B.** envious　　○ **C.** thrilled　　○ **D.** nervous

1. Use this Five W's chart to organize the key information associated with the historical event that is described in the last two paragraphs of this passage.

Who?	When?	Where?
What happened?		**Why was it important?**

2. Which of the Wright brothers was older, Wilbur or Orville? _____

3. The biggest problem in being able to fly a heavier-than-air flying machine was

_____

4. Why did the brothers think they were ready to build a powered airplane?

_____

5. Based on what you read, describe the *Flyer*. _____

_____

_____

6. What word do you think best describes how Orville must have felt when he got ready to take

off on the *Flyer*'s first flight? _____

Why do you think he felt this way?

_____

_____

The Write Stuff

Orville Wright once said, "Wilbur and I could hardly wait for morning to come to get at something that interests us. That's happiness!" What is something that makes you happy because it is very interesting or fun to do? Write about it in your journal or on a separate sheet of paper.

Eleanor Roosevelt

Little Eleanor Roosevelt seemed to have everything. She lived with her **affluent** parents in an elegant New York City townhouse that was staffed with servants. At her grandmother's country mansion, where she spent many of her summers, she had her own pony. Yet Eleanor was shy and lonely. She felt awkward and plain looking, and tried hard to win the approval of her beautiful but not very affectionate mother. By the time she was 10, both of her parents had died, and she was living with her strict grandmother.

In 1899, when she was nearly 15, Eleanor was sent to a boarding school in England. She began to gain confidence in herself and make friends more easily. After three happy years at the school, she **reluctantly** returned to her grandmother's home. It was time, her grandmother insisted, for Eleanor to be introduced to New York society at parties and teas.

By 1920 Eleanor was the mother of five children and the wife of Franklin D. Roosevelt, a rising politician. In August of that year, women won the right to vote. Eleanor, who had believed that politics was a man's business, soon became an active participant in the League of Women Voters. Eager to join the fight for social reform, she also worked tirelessly for organizations that were trying to end child labor and improve working conditions for women.

Eleanor's public life continued to grow. She helped Franklin campaign for the presidency and, in 1933, became the nation's First Lady. The country was in the grips of the Great Depression, a period of hard times and widespread unemployment that had started in 1929. Eleanor traveled all over the country to view conditions firsthand and reported her findings to Franklin. Particularly concerned about America's youth, she persuaded her husband to set up a special agency to provide job training and work projects for young people. Never afraid to champion unpopular issues, Eleanor became a strong supporter of racial equality. She met with African American leaders and spoke out against segregation and prejudice.

Franklin began his third term as President in 1941. Late in that year the United States entered World War II. Eleanor traveled to England and then to the South Pacific, where she visited American servicemen in their camps and comforted the wounded in hospitals. In 1945, shortly before the end of the war, Franklin died. Eleanor moved out of the White House, but she did not retire from public service. When the United Nations was established in October of that year, she was asked to be a delegate to its General Assembly. She served with the UN until 1953 and played a leading role in writing its Universal Declaration of Human Rights. This remarkable woman, who had once been so timid and shy, continued to stand up courageously for important issues and causes until her death in 1962.

1. **Based on what you read, you can conclude that when Eleanor was a young child she**
   - ○ **A.** was afraid of horses.
   - ○ **B.** had to help her mother with all of the household chores.
   - ○ **C.** didn't have very many friends.
   - ○ **D.** was admired for being very pretty.

2. **In the first paragraph, Eleanor's parents are described as being <u>affluent</u>. Which of these is the best synonym for *affluent*?**
   - ○ **A.** worried
   - ○ **B.** wealthy
   - ○ **C.** timid
   - ○ **D.** poor

3. **Why did her grandmother want Eleanor to return home after her third year at the boarding school in England?**
   - ○ **A.** She wanted her to attend a college in New York.
   - ○ **B.** She knew that she was unhappy at the school.
   - ○ **C.** She wanted her to start training for a career as a social worker.
   - ○ **D.** She wanted her to meet young people in New York's fashionable society.

4. **In paragraph two, it says that Eleanor "<u>reluctantly</u> returned to her grandmother's home." Which of these is the best antonym for *reluctantly*?**
   - ○ **A.** eagerly
   - ○ **B.** bravely
   - ○ **C.** politely
   - ○ **D.** patiently

5. **In what year did Franklin D. Roosevelt begin his first term as the nation's President?**
   - ○ **A.** 1941
   - ○ **B.** 1933
   - ○ **C.** 1929
   - ○ **D.** 1945

6. **During her years as First Lady, which of these did Eleanor Roosevelt NOT do?**
   - ○ **A.** meet with African American leaders
   - ○ **B.** play an important role in writing the Universal Declaration of Human Rights
   - ○ **C.** convince her husband to set up an agency to help the country's young people
   - ○ **D.** travel to the South Pacific to help raise the spirits of American servicemen

7. **When she was First Lady, with which of these statements would Eleanor Roosevelt most likely have agreed?**
   - ○ **A.** African American children and white children should have separate schools.
   - ○ **B.** Women should not be involved in politics.
   - ○ **C.** A First Lady's most important responsibility is to entertain White House guests.
   - ○ **D.** All people, regardless of race, should be treated with dignity.

8. **What is the main reason that Eleanor Roosevelt was so respected and admired?**
   - ○ **A.** She helped her husband campaign for the presidency.
   - ○ **B.** She belonged to the League of Women Voters.
   - ○ **C.** She spent her life trying to make the world a better place for others.
   - ○ **D.** She was the mother of five children.

Comprehension Homework Packets © 2007 by Jan Meyer Scholastic Teaching Resources

1. A number of important events in the history of the United States happened during Eleanor Roosevelt's lifetime. Complete the timeline below by filling in a short description of the historical events that happened in 1920, 1929, 1941, and 1945.

1920:		1941:	

1900	**1910**	**1920**	**1930**	**1940**	**1950**

1929:		1945:	

2. Why was Eleanor living with her grandmother by the time she was 10 years old?

_____

3. What was one of the causes for which Eleanor Roosevelt fought in the 1920s?

_____

4. With what world organization did Eleanor Roosevelt work after the death of her husband?

_____

5. When Eleanor was a child, she was shy and lonely. What two adjectives do you think best describe her as an adult?

_____

_____

6. Eleanor Roosevelt was a humanitarian. What do you think a *humanitarian* is? Take a good guess, then look it up in the dictionary to see if you're right.

My guess: _____

The dictionary definition in my own words: _____

_____

The Write Stuff

In her book *This Is My Life*, Eleanor Roosevelt wrote, "No one can make you feel inferior without your consent." In your journal or on a separate sheet of paper, write about what you think she meant and why you agree or disagree with her. Be sure to include at least one example to support your point of view.

The Statue of Liberty

On an evening in 1865 Édouard de Laboulaye gave a party at his home in France. He and his guests talked about the friendship between France and the United States and recalled that France had given aid to the American colonies in their Revolutionary War. "Wouldn't it be wonderful," Laboulaye exclaimed, "if France and the United States joined together to build a monument in America celebrating that nation's independence!" Frédéric-Auguste Bartholdi, a young sculptor and guest at the party, was **intrigued** by Laboulaye's idea. He believed that creating a monument for America would be a great project for him to undertake.

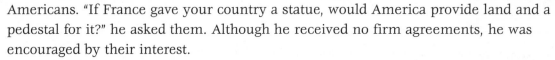

Hoping to promote Laboulaye's idea, Bartholdi went to the United States in 1871. As his ship entered New York Harbor, he saw tiny Bedloe's Island. What a perfect spot for the statue, he thought. Bartholdi stayed for five months, meeting with **prominent** Americans. "If France gave your country a statue, would America provide land and a pedestal for it?" he asked them. Although he received no firm agreements, he was encouraged by their interest.

Bartholdi returned to France and worked on his design for the statue—a gigantic figure of a robed woman holding up a shining torch in her right hand. He made sketches and clay models, but he would need money, he realized, to pay for Liberty's construction.

In 1875 a campaign was launched in France to raise funds for the statue. Bartholdi could now begin building his 151-foot-high figure. Meanwhile, in America, Congress agreed to accept the statue and to set aside Bedloe's Island for its site. Because Congress refused to approve funds for the pedestal, a committee was formed to raise the money. In 1881 Richard Morris Hunt was selected to design the pedestal, but fundraising went so slowly that its construction didn't begin until 1884.

By that same year, Liberty's copper skin and supporting inner skeleton of iron beams and bars stood completed and fastened together in a courtyard outside Bartholdi's workshop. She was the largest statue of her time, with a nose over four feet long and a mouth measuring three feet wide. In 1885 the statue was taken apart, packed in 214 crates, and shipped to Bedloe's Island. The crates sat there for nearly a year, waiting for the pedestal to be finished.

The dedication ceremony of the Statue of Liberty took place on October 28, 1886. There were parades, cannon blasts, and a speech by U.S. President Grover Cleveland. Bartholdi stood high up in the head of the statue, waiting to drop the enormous French flag that covered Liberty's face. When she was unveiled, the gathered crowds gazed in awe at this beautiful gift from France, a lasting memorial to America's freedom and liberty.

1. **In the first paragraph, it says that Bartholdi "was <u>intrigued</u> by Laboulaye's idea." Which of these is the best antonym for *intrigued*?**

   ○ **A.** disinterested   ○ **B.** angered   ○ **C.** amused   ○ **D.** discouraged

2. **What was the main reason that Bartholdi traveled to the United States in 1871?**

   ○ **A.** He wanted to raise money for the construction of the statue.

   ○ **B.** He wanted to attend the Statue of Liberty's dedication ceremony.

   ○ **C.** He wanted to look for a site for his statue.

   ○ **D.** He wanted to gain interest in a monument celebrating America's independence.

3. **In paragraph two, it says that Bartholdi met "with <u>prominent</u> Americans." Which of these is the best synonym for *prominent*?**

   ○ **A.** dishonest   ○ **B.** unfriendly   ○ **C.** important   ○ **D.** patient

4. **The Statue of Liberty's pedestal is made of concrete covered by blocks of granite. What is the statue's outer skin made of?**

   ○ **A.** wood   ○ **B.** copper   ○ **C.** marble   ○ **D.** clay

5. **Why did the crates containing the statue sit in America for nearly a year?**

   ○ **A.** Congress hadn't yet agreed to accept the statue.

   ○ **B.** Raising funds to put the statue back together went very slowly.

   ○ **C.** The construction of the pedestal had to be finished.

   ○ **D.** A designer for the pedestal still had to be chosen.

6. **Which of these men gave a speech at the Statue of Liberty's dedication ceremony?**

   ○ **A.** Frédéric-Auguste Bartholdi

   ○ **B.** Grover Cleveland

   ○ **C.** Édouard de Laboulaye

   ○ **D.** Richard Morris Hunt

7. **This passage on the Statue of Liberty is mostly about**

   ○ **A.** the process and materials used by Bartholdi to construct the Statue of Liberty.

   ○ **B.** the friendship between France and the United States.

   ○ **C.** the great size of the Statue of Liberty.

   ○ **D.** how Laboulaye's idea for a monument for America slowly became a reality.

8. **Which of these statements about the Statue of Liberty is NOT true?**

   ○ **A.** The statue's face was covered with an American flag at the dedication ceremony.

   ○ **B.** The statue's nose is over four feet long.

   ○ **C.** The statue's outer skin is supported by a skeleton of iron bars and beams.

   ○ **D.** The island on which the statue stands is very small.

1. More than 20 years passed between the year that Laboulaye proposed his idea of a monument celebrating America's independence and the year that the Statue of Liberty was dedicated. Fill in the timeline with important years and events in its history.

Year	Event
1865	

2. What example of the friendship between America and France did Laboulaye and his guests talk about at Laboulaye's party?

_____

_____

3. Where did Bartholdi's statue stand before it was taken apart and shipped to the United States?

_____

_____

4. What three synonyms for *large* are used in this passage about the Statue of Liberty?

_____

5. The island where the Statue of Liberty stands was renamed Liberty Island in 1956. What was the name of this island in 1886?

_____

6. The Statue of Liberty cradles a tablet in her left arm with the date July 4, 1776, on it. What important event in the history of America do you think is represented by this date?

_____

The Write Stuff

Pretend that you are an artist who has been asked to create a statue of an important figure in the history of the United States. In your journal or on a separate sheet of paper, write about who you would pick for your statue, why you would select this person, and where you would like your statue to stand.

Babe Ruth

Babe Ruth, named George Herman Ruth, Jr., by his parents, was born in 1895 in Baltimore, Maryland. His mother and father worked long hours at a tavern they owned and had little time for their son. Often left on his own, George rarely went to school. Instead, he liked to wander around the streets of his rundown, waterfront neighborhood. By the time George was 7 years old, his parents were fed up with trying to control their **unruly** son. They sent him off to St. Mary's Industrial School for Boys, a Catholic reform school and orphanage.

At St. Mary's, Brother Matthias, the school's head of discipline, helped George direct his restless energy into playing baseball. Before long, George could hit the ball harder and farther than many of the older boys. When he was about 15, he learned to be a pitcher. This was a position for which George, a left-hander, soon showed an extraordinary ability.

In 1914 George left St. Mary's with a contract to play for a minor league team. Because he was so young, his new teammates called him "Babe." This became the name that stuck with him for the rest of his life. That same year he was sold to the Boston Red Sox. At the age of 19, Babe Ruth had become a major league baseball player.

For the next six years, Ruth was a pitcher and then an outfielder for the Red Sox. In a 1916 World Series game against the Brooklyn Dodgers, he pitched 13 scoreless innings in a 14-inning game. The Red Sox won the game 2-1. His batting was even more amazing than his pitching. In 1919 he hit 29 home runs, breaking a record that had stood for 35 years.

Ruth was sold to the New York Yankees in January of 1920. In his first season as an outfielder for this club, he belted an incredible 54 home runs. Ruth's popularity soared. Thousands of **avid** fans came to the games, hoping to see him slam the ball into the bleachers. He drew so many fans that, in time, the Yankees could afford to build a stadium of their own. This new ballpark opened in 1923 and became known as "The House That Ruth Built."

Both on the field and off, Ruth had a colorful personality. He loved to eat and had a huge appetite. It's said that he once ate twelve hot dogs and drank eight sodas between games at a double header. He also loved children and spent endless hours visiting kids in hospitals and orphanages. Often acting like a kid himself, he became instant friends with his young fans.

One of the greatest sluggers of his time, Ruth set his famous record of 60 single-season home runs in 1927. In a game on May 25, 1935, days before he retired, he hit three homers, ending his 22 seasons as a major leaguer with 714 career home runs. This record remained unbroken for 39 years. In recognition of his exceptional talent, Babe Ruth was elected to the National Baseball Hall of Fame in 1936.

1. **In the first paragraph, George Ruth is described as an "unruly son." Which of these is the best antonym for *unruly*?**

   ○ **A.** handsome   ○ **B.** weak   ○ **C.** well-behaved   ○ **D.** clumsy

2. **Why did George Ruth's parents send their son to the St. Mary's Industrial School for Boys?**

   ○ **A.** They wanted him to learn how to play baseball.

   ○ **B.** They wanted him to learn about the Catholic religion.

   ○ **C.** They wanted him to learn about different industries.

   ○ **D.** They were tired of trying to handle his bad behavior.

3. **In what year did Ruth become a major league baseball player?**

   ○ **A.** 1916   ○ **B.** 1914   ○ **C.** 1919   ○ **D.** 1920

4. **For what team was Ruth playing in 1916?**

   ○ **A.** the Brooklyn Dodgers   ○ **B.** the Boston Red Sox

   ○ **C.** the Baltimore Orioles   ○ **D.** the New York Yankees

5. **In paragraph five, it describes Ruth's fans as <u>avid</u>. Which of these is the best synonym for *avid*?**

   ○ **A.** enthusiastic   ○ **B.** jealous   ○ **C.** amused   ○ **D.** clever

6. **Why did so many fans come to the Yankee games in the early 1920s?**

   ○ **A.** They wanted to sit in the bleachers.

   ○ **B.** They wanted to see Babe Ruth pitch scoreless innings.

   ○ **C.** They wanted to eat lots of hot dogs and drink lots of sodas.

   ○ **D.** They wanted to see Babe Ruth hit a home run.

7. **Based on what you read, which of these do you think Ruth would have been likely to order for breakfast in a restaurant?**

   ○ **A.** two slices of toast with butter and jam

   ○ **B.** a bowl of cereal with milk and sliced bananas

   ○ **C.** a steak, six fried eggs, and potatoes on the side

   ○ **D.** three pancakes with syrup and fresh strawberries

8. **Which of the following statements about Babe Ruth is true?**

   ○ **A.** He learned to be an outstanding outfielder at St. Mary's.

   ○ **B.** He was named "Babe" by his parents.

   ○ **C.** He played major league baseball for 39 seasons.

   ○ **D.** He set a new record by hitting 60 home runs in 1927.

1. The sports pages of newspapers use headlines to capture readers' attention. In the strips below, write three headlines about Babe Ruth that might have appeared in each of the years indicated. Be sure to make your headlines short, clear, and exciting.

1916

1920

1935

2. What word in paragraph one helps you to conclude that Ruth and his parents lived in a poor section of Baltimore?

_____

3. What did Brother Matthias do that influenced Ruth's life? _____

_____

4. Why did the Yankees new stadium become known as "The House That Ruth Built"?

_____

_____

5. What did Ruth do off the playing field that showed he was a warm, caring person?

_____

6. In 1914 Ruth became a rookie player for the Boston Red Sox. What do you think a *rookie* is? Take a good guess, then look it up in the dictionary to see if you're right.

My guess: _____

The dictionary definition in my own words: _____

_____

The Write Stuff

Babe Ruth once said, "Never let the fear of striking out get in your way." This is good advice for living one's life as well as for playing baseball. In your journal or on a separate sheet of paper, write about a time when you tried very hard to do something, even though you thought you might not be successful.

Walt Disney

Young Walt Disney loved to draw. One day, when he was 6 years old, he found a bucket of black gooey tar. Using a stick and the tar, he painted a large picture on the side of the white farmhouse where he lived. He didn't realize that when the tar dried it wouldn't come off!

In 1910 the Disneys moved to Kansas City where Walt's father became a newspaper distributor. Walt, now age 8, had to get up at 3:30 each morning to help deliver papers. "Your pay," stated his **stern** father, "is the home I provide for you." At school, Walt formed a close friendship with his classmate Walter Pfeiffer. The two boys put together comedy acts that they performed at amateur nights at theaters. Although he liked performing comedy, Walt's greatest joys were drawing cartoons and taking Saturday classes at the Art Institute.

By 1920 Walt was pursuing his dream of becoming a cartoonist. He accepted a job at Kansas City Film Ad, a company that created animated commercials for local businesses. These ads were made by using cut-out paper figures with movable joints. Walt became fascinated by animation and learned everything he could on the subject. Spending hours every night in his father's garage, he experimented with filming series of drawings—a technique the best animators were using. In 1922 he formed his own company that made animated cartoons called Laugh-O-Grams. Just one year later, though, his company went bankrupt. With almost no money left, 21-year-old Walt headed for Hollywood. In time he had a new company, Walt Disney Productions, that was creating Oswald the Lucky Rabbit cartoons.

On November 18, 1928, a new Disney cartoon titled Steamboat Willie opened in New York City. Billed in the program as "the FIRST animated cartoon with SOUND," it featured an **endearing** mouse named Mickey, whose voice had been done by Walt. The film was a huge hit. By 1934 Disney had produced more than 60 Mickey Mouse cartoons. The next year, the company used a new technology to make the first Mickey Mouse cartoon in color.

With his cartoon business now a success, Walt began looking for new challenges. He decided to produce America's first full-length animated film. It was to be based on the fairy tale Snow White. Walt supervised every step of the production, pushing everyone to meet his high standards. The film, which took three years to complete, had its first presentation on December 21, 1937. When the movie ended, the audience stood up and cheered.

Over the next 21 years, Walt built Walt Disney Productions into an empire of family entertainment. Working nonstop, he led his company into the production of live-action movies and television programming. In 1955 he realized his most ambitious dream when Disneyland opened in California. This extraordinary man, who brought joy and laughter to so many, died in 1966.

Comprehension Homework Packets © 2007 by Joe Moore & Joshua Tarkington

1. **Which of these words best describes the picture that Walt made on the side of his family's white farmhouse?**

   ○ **A.** permanent   ○ **B.** colorful   ○ **C.** animated   ○ **D.** tiny

2. **In paragraph two, Walt's father is described as** <u>stern</u>**. Which of these is the best synonym for** *stern*?

   ○ **A.** handsome   ○ **B.** strict   ○ **C.** generous   ○ **D.** lively

3. **When he was a young teenager, Walt helped create something called "The Two Walts." Based on what you read in this biography, you can conclude that this was**

   ○ **A.** a television program.   ○ **B.** an animated cartoon.

   ○ **C.** an animated commercial.   ○ **D.** a comedy act.

4. **According to what you read in this biography, which of these statements is true?**

   ○ **A.** The company that made Oswald the Lucky Rabbit cartoons went bankrupt.

   ○ **B.** Animated cartoons made before 1928 were silent and in black-and-white.

   ○ **C.** In 1920 the best animation was done using cut-out paper figures.

   ○ **D.** Laugh-O-Grams were animated commercials for Kansas City businesses.

5. **In paragraph four, it says that Steamboat Willie "featured an** <u>endearing</u> **mouse named Mickey." Which of these is the best synonym for** *endearing*?

   ○ **A.** lovable   ○ **B.** silent   ○ **C.** unpleasant   ○ **D.** scary

6. **What made Disney's** *Snow White and the Seven Dwarfs* **an important event in motion picture history?**

   ○ **A.** It was the first animated cartoon with sound.

   ○ **B.** It was America's first animated film in color.

   ○ **C.** It was America's first full-length animated film.

   ○ **D.** It was Disney's first live-action movie.

7. **Why was 1955 a very special year for Walt Disney?**

   ○ **A.** It was his first year in Hollywood.

   ○ **B.** His cartoon business had finally become a success.

   ○ **C.** His company had produced its fiftieth Mickey Mouse cartoon.

   ○ **D.** It was the year that Disneyland opened.

8. **Which of the following helped Walt Disney make his company so successful?**

   ○ **A.** He made sure that the films he produced met his high standards.

   ○ **B.** He worked very hard and looked for new challenges.

   ○ **C.** He used new technologies to make some of his films important "firsts."

   ○ **D.** all of the above

1. In the boxes below, create your own cartoon character. It can be an animal, a person, a superhero, or anything you'd like. Let your imagination run wild. Be sure to give your character a name.

Picture	**Written Description**

2. When Walt was 8 years old, he got up at 3:30 each morning. Why did he get up so early?

_____

3. What two childhood interests helped Walt in his career as a maker of animated cartoons?

_____

4. Whose voice was used for Mickey Mouse in the animated cartoon Steamboat Willie?

_____

5. Disney's hit film *Mary Poppins* had its premiere on August 27, 1964, at Grauman's Chinese Theater in Hollywood. What do you think *premiere* means? Take a good guess, then look it up in the dictionary to see if you're right.

My guess: _____

The dictionary definition in my own words: _____

_____

6. Why is *ambitious* a good word to describe Walt Disney?

_____

_____

The Write Stuff

What is your favorite animated film? In your journal or on a separate sheet of paper, write about this film. What is it about and why do you like it so much?

Cesar Chavez

When "Papa Chayo" Chavez migrated from Mexico to the United States, he never dreamed that one of his grandsons would become a famous labor leader. That grandson, Cesar Chavez, founded this country's first successful union for farm workers and helped bring these workers hope, justice, and respect.

Cesar was born in 1927 near Yuma, Arizona. His father owned a store and ran the family farm. He taught Cesar that it was important to stand up for his rights and the rights of others. Cesar's mother made sure that he understood that violence and rudeness were wrong.

In the 1930s the Depression brought hard times to the Chavez family. Cesar's father lost his store and then the farm. In 1938 they were forced to pack their belongings into their old car and head for California. There they joined the thousands of migrant farm workers who traveled from place to place looking for work wherever fruits or vegetables needed to be picked. Like other migrant workers, the Chavez family was often housed in rundown shacks with no bathroom, running water, or electricity. The backbreaking labor was very low paying and frequently lasted from sunup to sundown. Cesar went to school when and where he could, but he quit after the eighth grade to **toil** full-time in the fields.

Chavez dreamed of improving the lives of farm workers. In 1952 he began working for an organization that provided assistance to Mexican-Americans, many of whom worked in the fields. More and more convinced that farm workers could help themselves best by forming a union, Chavez left this job in 1962 to start the National Farm Workers Association (NFWA). He traveled around California talking to migrant workers and signing up members. By joining together, he explained, they would have more power.

In 1965 the NFWA began a strike against California grape growers to protest the poor treatment of the workers. The pickers came to the fields but refused to work. Some growers threatened them with shotguns and snarling dogs, but Chavez insisted that the strikers not use violence of any kind. To draw attention to their cause, Chavez led a 340-mile march to the state capital in 1966. College students, religious leaders, and hundreds of others joined the march. Then Chavez called for a boycott of grapes. He sent union representatives all over the United States, asking people not to buy California grapes until the pickers were treated fairly. Finally, by 1970, most of the grape growers had agreed to give the workers higher pay and better working conditions.

Chavez continued to lead the union in their struggle against farm owners. There were victories and setbacks, but he never gave up. In 1994, a year after his death, this dedicated and determined man was awarded the Presidential Medal of Freedom.

1. **Based on what you read in this biography, you can conclude that Cesar's father didn't buy and run a store when they went to California because**
   ○ **A.** California already had too many stores.
   ○ **B.** he preferred working on farms.
   ○ **C.** he had lost his savings and was now very poor.
   ○ **D.** he was tired of being a store owner because it was hard work.

2. **Which of these is the best synonym for** <u>toil</u> **as it is used in paragraph three?**
   ○ **A.** wander   ○ **B.** work   ○ **C.** teach   ○ **D.** study

3. **Cesar attended more than 30 different schools. From what you read, why do you think he changed schools so often?**
   ○ **A.** His mother kept looking for better schools for him to attend.
   ○ **B.** His family was constantly moving around the state.
   ○ **C.** He continually got into trouble.
   ○ **D.** He wanted to find a school where he could study farming.

4. **What had Chavez learned as a child that helped influence him to start a union for farm workers?**
   ○ **A.** It is wrong to be lazy.
   ○ **B.** It is important to work in the fields from sunup to sundown.
   ○ **C.** It is wrong to be rude.
   ○ **D.** It is important to stand up for your rights and the rights of others.

5. **In what year did Chavez start signing up members for the NFWA?**
   ○ **A.** 1962   ○ **B.** 1965   ○ **C.** 1952   ○ **D.** 1970

6. **Why do you think many of the leading grape growers did not want to pay higher wages to their grape pickers?**
   ○ **A.** They felt the work was very easy and didn't deserve higher pay.
   ○ **B.** They couldn't afford to pay the pickers more money.
   ○ **C.** They felt that many of the pickers were troublemakers.
   ○ **D.** They wanted to keep most of their profits for themselves.

7. **Why did the grape boycott help to pressure growers to accept the union's demands?**
   ○ **A.** Their workers were picking too many grapes.
   ○ **B.** They had to start making their grapes into jelly and juice.
   ○ **C.** They were making less money because sales of their grapes dropped.
   ○ **D.** They had to start advertising their grapes in newspapers and on television.

8. **What did Chavez help bring to farm workers?**
   ○ **A.** justice   ○ **B.** hope   ○ **C.** respect   ○ **D.** all of the above

1. Chavez believed that the living and working conditions of migrant farm workers were unpleasant and unfair. Can you find three examples in what you read that support this belief? Write these examples of unfair treatment in the chart below.

Belief	Examples
The living and working conditions of migrant farm workers were unpleasant and unfair.	1. 2. 3.

2. Who was "Papa Chayo" Chavez?

_____

3. Name five foods that you think might be picked by migrant farm workers.

_____

4. What were two ways that the union pressured grape growers to accept their demands?

_____

_____

5. Chavez and the union fought against grape growers who exploited their workers. What do you think *exploit* means in this sentence? Take a good guess, then look it up in the dictionary to see if you're right.

My guess: _____

The dictionary definition in my own words: _____

_____

6. Write at least three adjectives that describe what Chavez was like.

_____

The Write Stuff

Was there a time when you stood up for your rights or the rights of a friend? Write about it in your journal or on a separate sheet of paper.

The Dust Bowl

Lured by the federal government's offer of free land, thousands of settlers established farms on the Great Plains in the late 1800s. By 1920 millions of acres of prairie grassland had been plowed under and planted in wheat. More powerful tractors and increasing crop yields made opportunities for successful farming seem unlimited. In the 1930s, however, many Great Plains farmers lost everything they had worked for. It had stopped raining!

There had been long periods without rain in the Great Plains before, but this drought started in 1931 and lasted for eight years! Crops withered and died. The soil, weakened by years of overplowing and poor farming practices, turned into dust. In 1932 dust storms began hitting the area. With few crop roots and grasses to hold the ground in place, strong prairie winds whipped the dusty soil out of the fields and into the air. A particularly powerful storm struck in May 1934. It carried tons of powdery dirt all the way to East Coast cities. Even ships hundreds of miles out in the Atlantic Ocean were covered with dust.

Year after year dust storms filled the air with stinging dirt. These "black blizzards" swept in without warning and changed day into night. Once a storm ended, dirt had to be shoveled away from barn doors, off of farm equipment, and out of houses. There was dirt and dust everywhere—on furniture, on clothes, on dishes, and even in the food. Because breathing the air could be dangerous, families slept with wet cloths over their noses and mouths. In spite of such measures, cases of asthma, bronchitis, and "dust pneumonia" soared.

Hardest hit by the drought and the dust storms was the southern Great Plains, an area that included large sections of Oklahoma, Texas, Kansas, Colorado, and New Mexico. Ponds dried up, cows died of starvation and thirst, and much of the **arid** farmland could no longer produce crops. There was so much damage that this area became known as the Dust Bowl.

Defeated by poverty from repeated crop failures, large numbers of Dust Bowl farm families packed up their belongings and headed west for California. There were lots of jobs there, they'd been told, picking fruits and vegetables. They arrived filled with **optimism** but soon discovered there were thousands of poor people looking for work and few available jobs. Many found that their lives in California were just as hard as the lives they had left behind.

In 1939 rain began to fall again in the Great Plains. By then, many farmers had started to use planting and plowing methods that would protect and enrich the soil. They had learned from government-sponsored programs to rotate crops, reseed some areas with grasses, and plant trees to break the wind. Using responsible farming practices, they now knew, would prevent such a disaster from happening again.

1. **What evidence is given in this passage that the dust storm in May 1934 was particularly strong?**
   - ○ **A.** Farmers had to shovel dirt off of their farm equipment.
   - ○ **B.** Crops withered and died in the fields.
   - ○ **C.** Cases of asthma, bronchitis, and "dust pneumonia" soared.
   - ○ **D.** Ships out in the Atlantic Ocean were covered in dust.

2. **In paragraph three, it says that the dust storms "changed day into night." This phrase means that**
   - ○ **A.** farm families hid from the storms in their beds.
   - ○ **B.** the storms lasted all through the night.
   - ○ **C.** the thick, swirling dust made the sky as dark as night.
   - ○ **D.** clocks were affected by the storms.

3. **Why did people sleep with wet cloths over their noses and mouths?**
   - ○ **A.** It was very hot in their bedrooms.
   - ○ **B.** They thought it would prevent them from snoring.
   - ○ **C.** The cloths helped to screen out the dust in the air.
   - ○ **D.** The air was very dry because it hadn't rained for a long time.

4. **Which of these was NOT one of the states in the Dust Bowl?**
   - ○ **A.** California   ○ **B.** Oklahoma   ○ **C.** Kansas   ○ **D.** Texas

5. **In paragraph four, it describes the Dust Bowl farmland as <u>arid</u>. Which of these is the best synonym for *arid*?**
   - ○ **A.** rocky   ○ **B.** dry   ○ **C.** rich   ○ **D.** moist

6. **In paragraph five, it says that Dust Bowl families arrived in California "filled with <u>optimism</u>." Which of these is the best antonym for *optimism*?**
   - ○ **A.** enthusiasm   ○ **B.** selfishness   ○ **C.** hopelessness   ○ **D.** shame

7. **By 1939 many Great Plains farmers had learned that**
   - ○ **A.** poor farming practices can cause it to stop raining.
   - ○ **B.** wheat should not be grown in the Great Plains.
   - ○ **C.** they should keep their houses clean and dusted.
   - ○ **D.** they must protect their soil by using responsible farming practices.

8. **Based on what you read in this passage, which of these statements is true?**
   - ○ **A.** The first drought that the Great Plains had ever experienced started in 1931.
   - ○ **B.** By 1920 much of the Great Plains' prairie grasses were gone.
   - ○ **C.** There were lots of jobs in California for Dust Bowl farm families.
   - ○ **D.** The eastern Great Plains was the hardest hit by the drought and the dust storms.

1. Cause-and-effect relationships explain why actions and events happen and why decisions are made. In each row below, fill in the missing cause (reason why) or effect (what happened or resulted).

CAUSE	EFFECT
The federal government offered free land to anyone who would settle on it and develop it.	
There were few crop roots and grasses to hold the ground in place.	
	Many Dust Bowl farm families packed up their possessions and headed for California.

2. What is a drought?

   _____

3. Why do you think the dust storms were called "black blizzards"?

   _____

   _____

4. A Dust Bowl farmer reported that "after the storm we had to climb out a window because we couldn't push open the front door." Why do you think they couldn't open the door?

   _____

5. Why did many Dust Bowl farm families think that California might be a good place to begin a new life?

   _____

   _____

6. Why did government-sponsored programs advise farmers to plant trees?

   _____

   _____

The Write Stuff

Weather can often affect our day-to-day lives. It can make us feel happy or gloomy, help or harm the environment, and influence the kinds of things we do outdoors. In your journal or on a separate sheet of paper, make a list of at least ten ways in which weather can make your day fun or help the environment. Then make a list of at least ten ways in which weather can spoil your fun or harm the environment.

Rosie the Riveter

In the 1940s, the United States was fighting in World War II. Men were being sent off to war. They were leaving well-paying jobs in the manufacturing industry. Soon there was a labor **shortage** and the country had to make major changes. The Office of War Information introduced an ad campaign to attract women to the workforce.

Posters and advertisements showed a woman with a red bandanna on her head. She wore overalls and a shirt with her sleeves rolled up, flexing her muscles. The woman became known as Rosie the Riveter. Her image was used to get women to fill in for men who were fighting in the war.

Before World War II, most women who worked were single and young. Most of them worked as seamstresses. Married women were expected to stay at home. They were not supposed to worry about what was happening in the world. But World War II changed America's attitude about women. Rosie became the symbol of patriotic women who were doing what they could to help in the war effort.

Working outside of the home doing "men's work" was a new experience for many women. But they were up to the challenge. "An American homemaker with the strength and ability to run a house and raise a family . . . has the strength and ability to take her place in a **vital** War industry," one ad said. Another ad read, "Do the Job He Left Behind."

The Rosie the Riveter ad campaign featured Rosie with the slogan "We Can Do It!" And millions of women proved that they could do it. They worked in airplane plants and shipyards as steelworkers, riveters, and welders. Rosie's image was a huge success. By 1944, more than 19 million women had put down their aprons and picked up toolboxes to work for their country. Women were doing the "manly" jobs very well.

Many women enjoyed working outside the home. They developed a sense of pride and dignity in the work they were doing for their country. Some women even wanted to pursue a career after the war. But when the war ended in 1945, women were turned away from manufacturing jobs. Men returning from war wanted their jobs back. Many people believed that women should go back to raising children and being housewives. But the Rosie the Riveter campaign had created a new generation of women.

Thanks largely to the millions of dedicated women during World War II, women now work in all fields, including the engineering, manufacturing, medical, government, and defense industries. They work in jobs once held only by men. More important, women make the choice to work or stay at home, not the United States government. Women take great pride in their skill to work in many different types of jobs.

1. **Before World War II, which of the following characteristics describes a typical woman who worked outside of the home?**

   ○ **A.** young   ○ **B.** not married   ○ **C.** able to sew   ○ **D.** all of the above

2. **During World War II, the United States experienced a labor <u>shortage</u>. An antonym for *shortage* is**

   ○ **A.** tall   ○ **B.** lack of   ○ **C.** peace   ○ **D.** abundance

3. **How many American women entered the workforce during World War II?**

   ○ **A.** 1,945   ○ **B.** less than 10 thousand
   ○ **C.** more than 19 million   ○ **D.** 145 million

4. **Paragraph four says that women were encouraged to join a "<u>vital</u> War industry." What does the word *vital* mean?**

   ○ **A.** small   ○ **B.** not very important
   ○ **C.** very important   ○ **D.** busy

5. **Rosie the Riveter was introduced to the American public by**

   ○ **A.** The Office of Working Women
   ○ **B.** The U.S. Labor Committee
   ○ **C.** The Office of War Information
   ○ **D.** The Society of Former Homemakers

6. **Based on what you read, you can conclude that after World War II ended,**

   ○ **A.** all women were glad to return to working at home.
   ○ **B.** society experienced few changes.
   ○ **C.** women gained more control over their own lives.
   ○ **D.** people stopped paying attention to advertising.

7. **This passage about Rosie the Riveter is mostly about**

   ○ **A.** how women's roles in society have changed over time.
   ○ **B.** why women work outside of the home.
   ○ **C.** how to solve labor shortages.
   ○ **D.** steelworkers.

8. **The best word to describe the women you read about in this passage is**

   ○ **A.** fearful   ○ **B.** capable
   ○ **C.** uncooperative   ○ **D.** wealthy

1. Rosie the Riveter was a fictional character created by the federal government to encourage women to join the workforce during World War II. Create a character and design an ad to get people today to do something important.

2. Why do you think Rosie the Riveter was wearing a bandanna and overalls in the advertisement?

   _____

   _____

   _____

   _____

   _____

3. During World War II, where did many women begin to work?

   _____

   _____

   What kinds of jobs did they hold?

   _____

   _____

4. Why were women turned away from manufacturing jobs in 1945?

   _____

   _____

5. Rosie the Riveter became a "symbol of patriotic women." What do you think a *symbol* is? Take a good guess, then look it up in the dictionary to see if you're right.

   My guess: _____

   The dictionary definition in my own words: _____

   _____

The Write Stuff

Many women developed a sense of pride and dignity in the work they were doing for their country. In your journal or on a separate sheet of paper, write about something that gives you a sense of pride and dignity.

The Montgomery Bus Boycott

On Thursday, December 1, 1955, Rosa Parks waited for a bus at Court Square in Montgomery, Alabama. She was on her way home from her job as a seamstress at the Montgomery Fair, a department store. When the bus came, Parks, an African American, walked to the rear of the bus and sat down in the first row of the "colored section"—the section where black people were required to sit. By the next stop all of the seats became filled, and a white man was left standing. The bus driver demanded that Parks give her seat to the man, but she refused. She was tired of the **demeaning** treatment of black passengers. The driver sent for two policemen who arrested Parks and took her to jail.

Word of Parks' arrest spread quickly through the black community. Its leaders decided to call a one-day boycott of the buses on Monday, December 5, the day of Mrs. Parks' trial. Fliers asking Montgomery's African Americans to stay off the buses were distributed, and plans for alternate methods of transportation were set up. On Sunday, the city's black ministers called upon members of their churches to take part in the protest.

At her Monday morning trial, Parks was found guilty of breaking the bus segregation laws and fined ten dollars. That afternoon the leaders of the boycott formed the Montgomery Improvement Association (MIA) with Martin Luther King, Jr., as its president. The city buses had very few black riders that day. Eager to join the boycott, many African Americans rode in car pools or piled into black-owned taxis for a fare of ten cents. Others decided to walk.

A community meeting was held Monday night. Hundreds attended and voted to continue the boycott until the bus company agreed to treat black passengers fairly and with courtesy. Dr. King spoke to the crowd and urged them to work together and to protest peacefully.

Montgomery's black population of about 50,000 stayed off the buses month after month. The bus company started losing thousands of dollars, but its officers refused to meet the MIA's demands. As the boycott continued, the police began **harassing** the black drivers of car pools and taxis. Hate groups, like the White Citizens Council, made threatening phone calls and sent nasty letters to leading black citizens. Dr. King's home was fire-bombed. Through it all, though, the boycotters and the MIA leaders remained determined, united, and nonviolent.

It was through the federal courts that the MIA finally achieved a resolution and victory. On November 13, 1956, the U.S. Supreme Court ruled that segregated seating on Montgomery's public buses was unconstitutional. When the written court order arrived in Montgomery in December, the boycott ended. Black passengers, thanks in great part to Rosa Parks' courageous stand against injustice, could now ride the city buses and sit with dignity anywhere they wanted.

1. **Why did the bus driver have Rosa Parks arrested?**
   - ○ **A.** She was sitting in the front of the bus.
   - ○ **B.** She refused to give her seat to a white passenger.
   - ○ **C.** She had not paid her fair of ten cents.
   - ○ **D.** She had been rude to him.

2. **In paragraph one, it says that Parks was "tired of the <u>demeaning</u> treatment of black passengers." To *demean* a person means to**
   - ○ **A.** bore that person with uninteresting conversation.
   - ○ **B.** cause that person to lose pride or self-esteem.
   - ○ **C.** force that person to stop eating his or her snacks.
   - ○ **D.** confuse that person by giving wrong directions.

3. **Which of these words do you think best describes how Montgomery's black leaders probably felt when Parks was arrested?**
   - ○ **A.** ashamed
   - ○ **B.** frightened
   - ○ **C.** helpless
   - ○ **D.** angry

4. **At the community meeting on Monday night, it was decided that**
   - ○ **A.** the boycott should continue until the bus company changed its rules.
   - ○ **B.** Martin Luther King, Jr., should be the president of the MIA.
   - ○ **C.** black-owned taxis should charge a fare of ten cents.
   - ○ **D.** black passengers should pay more money to ride the city buses.

5. **In paragraph five, it says that "the police began <u>harassing</u> the black drivers of car pools and taxis." To *harass* means to**
   - ○ **A.** offer assistance.
   - ○ **B.** praise.
   - ○ **C.** bother repeatedly.
   - ○ **D.** disappoint.

6. **Based on what you read in this passage, you can conclude that members of the White Citizens Council**
   - ○ **A.** were pleased with the Supreme Court's decision.
   - ○ **B.** offered help and encouragement to Montgomery's leading black citizens.
   - ○ **C.** were in favor of the bus boycott.
   - ○ **D.** supported segregated seating on Montgomery's buses.

7. **Which of these statements about the Montgomery bus boycott is NOT true?**
   - ○ **A.** It caused the bus company to lose thousands of dollars.
   - ○ **B.** It inspired Montgomery's black community to become united.
   - ○ **C.** It was ruled unconstitutional by the U.S. Supreme Court.
   - ○ **D.** It brought about violence and threats from white hate groups.

8. **How long did the Montgomery bus boycott last?**
   - ○ **A.** one day
   - ○ **B.** about one year
   - ○ **C.** several months
   - ○ **D.** about two years

1. In the space below, create a two-page, attention-getting flyer announcing Montgomery's one-day bus boycott. Be sure to include when it will take place, why it is being held, and why everyone should participate.

2. Rosa Parks lost her job about one month after the beginning of the boycott. Where had she been working?

_____

3. What were three ways that Montgomery's African Americans got where they needed to go during the boycott?

_____

_____

4. About how many African Americans were living in Montgomery at the time of the bus boycott?

_____

5. Martin Luther King, Jr., believed in and encouraged others to use nonviolent resistance. What do you think the term *nonviolent resistance* means

_____

6. Why do you think that Parks' stand against injustice is described as courageous?

_____

_____

The Write Stuff

Martin Luther King, Jr., once said, "Our lives begin to end the day we become silent about things that matter." In your journal or on a separate sheet of paper, write about what you think he meant and why you agree or disagree with his words.

The *Apollo 11* Moon Landing

Thousands of people were gathered at Cape Kennedy, Florida, on the morning of July 16, 1969. They were there to witness the launch of *Apollo 11*, the first space mission designed to land astronauts on the moon and return them safely to Earth. Just eight years earlier, President John F. Kennedy had pledged that the United States would achieve this **unprecedented**, risk-filled feat before the end of the **decade**.

The towering, three-stage Saturn V rocket, standing 36 stories high, sat on the launch pad. In position above the rocket were the spacecraft's lunar module, service module, and command module. Inside the cone-shaped command module, the *Apollo 11* astronauts were strapped into their seats, preparing for liftoff. They were Neil Armstrong, mission commander; "Buzz" Aldrin, lunar module pilot; and Michael Collins, command module pilot.

At 9:32 A.M., with the engines of the Saturn V rocket's first stage at full power, *Apollo 11* blasted off with a thunderous roar. After one and a half orbits around the Earth, the rocket's third stage sent the spacecraft off on its journey to the moon.

On July 19, after traveling nearly 250,000 miles, *Apollo 11* began its orbit around the moon. On July 20, the fifth day of the mission, Armstrong and Aldrin entered the lunar module (named *Eagle*) and separated it from the command/service module (named *Columbia*). They fired *Eagle*'s descent engine and started down to the moon. Suddenly seeing that they were headed for a field of boulders, Armstrong quickly switched from computer control to manual control. He anxiously searched for a more suitable landing spot. At last, with less than 30 seconds of fuel remaining, *Eagle* touched down safely on a dusty plain called the Sea of Tranquility. Armstrong immediately radioed Mission Control in Houston, Texas. "Houston, Tranquility Base here. The *Eagle* has landed," he proudly announced.

Wearing a bulky spacesuit, a helmet, and a backpack life-support system, Armstrong descended *Eagle's* ladder. A special television camera allowed millions of people on Earth to watch as he made the first human footprint on the moon. Speaking with excitement, Armstrong declared that this was one small step for a man, but "one giant leap for mankind."

For about two hours Armstrong and Aldrin walked on the moon's powdery surface, setting up experiments and collecting samples of rocks and soil. The following day, July 21, they lifted off from the moon, docked *Eagle* with *Columbia*, and rejoined Collins who had been circling the moon in the command module. The astronauts were ready to head home.

On July 24 the command module splashed down in the Pacific Ocean, southwest of Hawaii. With bravery and skillful teamwork, the *Apollo 11* astronauts had accomplished their heroic mission.

1. **On July 16, 1969, thousands of people were at Cape Kennedy to**

   ○ **A.** witness the splashdown of *Apollo 11's* command module.

   ○ **B.** hear President John F. Kennedy make a speech.

   ○ **C.** watch Neil Armstrong take his first step on the moon.

   ○ **D.** see the liftoff of *Apollo 11*.

2. **In 1961 President John F. Kennedy pledged that the United States would land a man on the moon before the end of the <u>decade</u>. How long is a *decade*?**

   ○ **A.** 10 years   ○ **B.** 100 years   ○ **C.** 1 year   ○ **D.** 50 years

3. **In paragraph one, the feat of landing astronauts on the moon and returning them safely to Earth is described as being <u>unprecedented</u>. *Unprecedented* means**

   ○ **A.** very amusing to do.   ○ **B.** very easy to do.

   ○ **C.** never been done before.   ○ **D.** against the law.

4. **What was Michael Collins's job on the *Apollo 11* mission?**

   ○ **A.** He was the command module pilot.

   ○ **B.** He was the lunar module pilot.

   ○ **C.** He was in charge of Mission Control in Houston, Texas.

   ○ **D.** He was the *Apollo 11* mission commander.

5. **The Sea of Tranquility is**

   ○ **A.** a large body of water on the moon.

   ○ **B.** the place where *Apollo 11* splashed down when it returned from the moon.

   ○ **C.** a dusty plain on the surface of the moon.

   ○ **D.** the name of the three-stage rocket that powered the spacecraft on liftoff.

6. **On which day of its mission did the *Apollo 11* spacecraft begin to orbit around the moon?**

   ○ **A.** the fifth day   ○ **B.** the fourth day

   ○ **C.** the first day   ○ **D.** the sixth day

7. **Which of these statements about the *Apollo 11* mission is NOT true?**

   ○ **A.** Aldrin was the second human to step onto the surface of the moon.

   ○ **B.** *Eagle* had to separate from *Columbia* before it could begin its trip down to the moon.

   ○ **C.** Armstrong radioed Mission Control on July 20 to report that the *Eagle* had landed.

   ○ **D.** To avoid landing on boulders, Armstrong switched *Eagle* to computer control.

8. **The *Apollo 11* command module is now at the Smithsonian's National Air and Space Museum in Washington, D.C. It is shaped like a**

   ○ **A.** cylinder.   ○ **B.** cube.

   ○ **C.** cone.   ○ **D.** sphere.

Comprehension Homework Packets © 2007 by Jan Meyer Scholastic Teaching Resources

1. Newspapers use headlines to capture readers' attention. In the strips below, write three headlines about the *Apollo 11* mission that might have appeared on each of the dates shown below. Be sure to make your headlines short and exciting.

> **July 16, 1969**
>
> **July 20, 1969**
>
> **July 24, 1969**

2. In which of the spacecraft's modules did Armstrong and Aldrin land on the moon?

   _____

3. Where was Michael Collins while Armstrong and Aldrin were walking on the moon?

   _____

4. What do you think Neil Armstrong meant when he said that his small step on the moon was "one giant leap for mankind"?

   _____

   _____

5. What word do you think best describes how Armstrong must have felt when he stepped

   onto the moon? _____ Why do you think he felt that way?

   _____

   _____

6. What did Aldrin and Armstrong do while they were on the moon? _____

   _____

   _____

The Write Stuff

If Neil Armstrong hadn't reacted quickly, the lunar module might have crashed into boulders. Has fast thinking ever helped you avoid a problem or succeed in doing something? Write about it in your journal or on a separate sheet of paper.

Arachne

There once lived a young country girl named Arachne, who was a very talented weaver. She had learned this craft from Athena, the goddess of wisdom and teacher of the arts of spinning, weaving, and needlework. People came from miles around to admire Arachne's work, and she soon became quite conceited. "My weaving is even more beautiful than that of the goddess Athena," she boasted to her visitors.

Hearing this, Athena was **indignant**. Disguised as an old woman, she went down to earth to scold Arachne. "Be careful," she warned. "It is wrong to compare yourself to a goddess."

"But I am a better weaver," the girl haughtily insisted. "Let Athena come, if she dares, and we'll have a competition."

With that, the old woman disappeared. In her place stood the radiant, gray-eyed goddess Athena, crowned with her golden helmet. "Let the contest begin," she said. "We'll soon see who is more skilled."

Arachne and Athena sat down at their looms and began to weave. With shimmering threads of gold and silver, Athena wove wondrous pictures of the gods in all their glory. In the corners of her tapestry, she designed scenes of the punishments of mortals who had dared to compete with the gods. "Take note, foolish girl, before it's too late," she cautioned Arachne.

But Arachne paid no attention. Her shuttle, strung with rainbow-colored thread, flew back and forth across her loom. She smiled to herself as she filled her tapestry with scenes showing the gods' weaknesses, trickery, and faults.

When Athena saw Arachne's work, she was furious. "Your weaving is indeed skillfully done, but your pictures are an insult to the gods. You will pay for your arrogance and your lack of respect," she declared angrily.

The goddess took her shuttle and ripped the girl's tapestry to pieces. Then, she sprinkled Arachne with a magical liquid. The girl's body shrank and shrank until it was no bigger than a pebble. Her **agile** fingers, which had been so clever at weaving, turned into eight thin legs. Athena had transformed Arachne into a spider. "For all your days you will weave and spin," said the goddess, "and so will your children and your children's children."

1. **Athena's main purpose in coming to earth to visit Arachne was to**
   - ○ **A.** see if Arachne's weaving skills were truly better than hers.
   - ○ **B.** give her another weaving lesson.
   - ○ **C.** have a weaving competition with her.
   - ○ **D.** scold her for boasting about being a better weaver.

2. **According to the myth, which of these skills was Athena most likely to teach to women?**
   - ○ **A.** how to write poetry
   - ○ **B.** how to embroider fabric
   - ○ **C.** how to play a musical instrument
   - ○ **D.** how to paint portraits

3. **In what way were Athena and Arachne alike?**
   - ○ **A.** They were both mortals.
   - ○ **B.** They both had gray eyes.
   - ○ **C.** They were both very proud of their weaving skills.
   - ○ **D.** They both had magical powers.

4. **In paragraph two, it says, "Athena was <u>indignant</u>." Which of these is the best synonym for *indignant*?**
   - ○ **A.** puzzled
   - ○ **B.** astonished
   - ○ **C.** displeased
   - ○ **D.** afraid

5. **During the competition, Athena cautioned Arachne to take note before it was too late. What did the goddess want the girl to notice?**
   - ○ **A.** the scenes in her tapestry that showed the fate of mortals who tried to outdo the gods
   - ○ **B.** that she was wearing a golden helmet
   - ○ **C.** the shimmering gold and silver threads that she was using in her tapestry
   - ○ **D.** that her weaving was nearly finished

6. **In paragraph eight, Arachne's fingers are described as <u>agile</u>. Which of these is the best antonym for *agile*?**
   - ○ **A.** skillful
   - ○ **B.** strong
   - ○ **C.** wrinkled
   - ○ **D.** clumsy

7. **What emotion did Arachne seem to express while she was weaving her tapestry?**
   - ○ **A.** disappointment
   - ○ **B.** confidence
   - ○ **C.** boredom
   - ○ **D.** sadness

8. **Some myths have a moral (a lesson to be learned from the story). Which of these is the best moral for this myth?**
   - ○ **A.** Having talent can lead to trouble.
   - ○ **B.** Some spiders have a poisonous bite.
   - ○ **C.** Becoming a good weaver requires lots of practice.
   - ○ **D.** Being boastful and arrogant can lead to trouble.

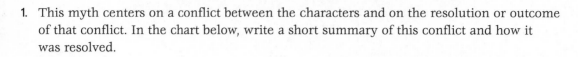
1. This myth centers on a conflict between the characters and on the resolution or outcome of that conflict. In the chart below, write a short summary of this conflict and how it was resolved.

CONFLICT	RESOLUTION

2. Why didn't Arachne recognize Athena when she first came to the girl's home?

   _____

3. What two pieces of weaving equipment are named in this story?

   _____

4. Why did Athena say that Arachne's pictures were "an insult to the gods"?

   _____

   _____

5. What special ability of spiders does this myth explain? _____

   _____

6. The word part *phobia* means "fear of." What do you think *arachnophobia* means? Take a good guess, then look it up in the dictionary to see if you're right.

   My guess: _____

   The dictionary definition in my own words: _____

   _____

The Write Stuff

Can you recall a time when someone's boasting made you mad? Write about it in your journal or on a separate sheet of paper.

Atalanta

When Atalanta was born, her father, King Iasus, was extremely disappointed. He had wanted a son. "Take this baby up into the mountains and leave her there," he ordered.

Fortunately, Atalanta was found by a mother bear that fed her and kept her warm. In time, some kind-hearted hunters discovered her and took her to live with them in their home. Atalanta grew to be strong and full of spirit. By the time she was a young woman, she could run more swiftly than a deer and shoot an arrow farther than many men.

One day Atalanta heard that heroes from all over Greece were going to Calydon to try to kill a ferocious wild boar. Eager for adventure, she set out to take part in the hunt. When she reached Calydon and joined the men in the forest, some of the heroes were **disgruntled**. "How insulting!" they shouted. "We won't hunt with a woman." But Prince Meleager, the son of Calydon's king, insisted that Atalanta was welcome.

Suddenly, the enormous boar came crashing through the trees, killing those who were nearest with its sharp tusks. Spears and arrows flew again and again, but all of them missed the beast. Atalanta, taking careful aim, shot an arrow. It struck the boar just behind its ear. Meleager rushed forward and killed the wounded boar with a spear. Although a few men objected, the prince awarded the boar's head to Atalanta for being the first to hit the beast.

Soon after Atalanta's triumph at Calydon, King Iasus proudly **reclaimed** his daughter. He was pleased that she was so brave and so bold. Atalanta received many proposals of marriage, but she had no interest in being married. To scare away her suitors, she came up with a plan. "I will wed the man who can beat me in a race. But anyone who loses must die," she declared.

In spite of the risk, a number of men agreed to race against Atalanta. All lost their lives. Then a young man named Hippomenes came to Iasus's palace. Aphrodite, the goddess of love, had given him three golden apples to help him win both the race and Atalanta's heart.

The next morning a signal sounded and their race began. As Atalanta sped ahead of him, Hippomenes tossed two of the apples in front of her. Unable to resist their golden gleam, she stopped and picked them up. Hippomenes dashed past her. But with a burst of speed, Atalanta was ahead of him again. They neared the end of the course, and Hippomenes threw the last apple far off to her side. Atalanta hesitated and then darted after it. Gasping for breath, Hippomenes joyously threw himself across the finish line.

Realizing that she had lost the race, Atalanta looked down at the glittering apples cupped in her hands. Then she looked over at Hippomenes. She slowly began to smile at the thought of having such a handsome and clever man as her husband.

1. **Why did King Iasus have Atalanta taken up into the mountains?**
   - ○ **A.** He wanted her to learn to hunt.
   - ○ **B.** He wanted to protect her from the wild boar of Calydon.
   - ○ **C.** He had no interest in raising a daughter.
   - ○ **D.** He wanted her to find a husband.

2. **Based on what you read in this myth, which of these skills do you think Atalanta was most likely to have learned from the hunters who raised her?**
   - ○ **A.** how to use a compass
   - ○ **B.** how to make clothes out of bear skins
   - ○ **C.** how to shoot with a bow and arrow
   - ○ **D.** how to make baskets out of twigs

3. **Why did Atalanta decide to go to Calydon?**
   - ○ **A.** She wanted to be reunited with her father.
   - ○ **B.** She wanted to do something adventurous.
   - ○ **C.** She wanted to marry Meleager.
   - ○ **D.** She wanted to race against the heroes.

4. **In paragraph three, it says that some of the heroes were <u>disgruntled</u> when they saw Atalanta. Which of these is the best synonym for *disgruntled*?**
   - ○ **A.** annoyed
   - ○ **B.** respectful
   - ○ **C.** alarmed
   - ○ **D.** confused

5. **Meleager thought that Atalanta deserved to be awarded the boar's head because**
   - ○ **A.** she had killed the beast with her arrow.
   - ○ **B.** she was the last to arrive at the hunt.
   - ○ **C.** she was the only woman in the hunting party.
   - ○ **D.** she was the first of the hunters to strike the beast.

6. **In paragraph five, it says that the king <u>reclaimed</u> his daughter. The word *reclaim* starts with the prefix *re*. Which of these is the meaning of this prefix?**
   - ○ **A.** before
   - ○ **B.** again
   - ○ **C.** against
   - ○ **D.** after

7. **Why was Hippomenes able to win his race against Atalanta?**
   - ○ **A.** He was a faster runner than Atalanta.
   - ○ **B.** He was helped by her father, King Iasus.
   - ○ **C.** He slowed Atalanta down by hitting her with golden apples.
   - ○ **D.** He was helped by the goddess Aphrodite.

8. **Which of these adjectives best describes how Atalanta felt when she realized that Hippomenes had won the race?**
   - ○ **A.** resentful
   - ○ **B.** happy
   - ○ **C.** sad
   - ○ **D.** ashamed

1. In the boxes below, illustrate three events in Atalanta's life. Be sure to put the events in the order in which they happened. Write a caption at the bottom of each of your drawings that tells briefly about the event.

    [ ] [ ] [ ]

    _____ _____ _____

2. What is one way in which Atalanta's childhood might have been different if she had grown up in a palace rather than in the mountains with the hunters?

    _____

    _____

3. According to the myth, what animal could Atalanta outrun?

    _____

4. Why do you think that a few of the men objected when Meleager awarded the boar's head to Atalanta?

    _____

    _____

5. With what weapon was the boar of Calydon killed?

    _____

6. What did Hippomenes do that caused Atalanta to think that he was clever?

    _____

    _____

The Write Stuff

Atalanta was as swift as the wind. So was Wilma Rudolph when she won three gold medals in the 1960 Olympics. Find out about the life of this champion Olympics runner, using the Internet or a reference book. In your journal or on a separate sheet of paper, write a report on what you learned about this amazing woman.

Bellerophon

Bellerophon, a prince from Corinth, came to the palace of Iobates, king of Lycia, with a sealed letter. "It's a letter of introduction from King Proetus," Bellerophon told Iobates.

The king welcomed the handsome young man and entertained him for many days before remembering to open the letter. When at last he did read it, he was astonished. It said, "Bellerophon is a brave youth. But I ask you to kill him, for he has greatly offended my wife."

Iobates wondered what he should do. To harm a guest in his palace would anger the gods. Yet King Proetus was his son-in-law, and, because of this, he was obliged to honor his request. After much thought, Iobates came up with a solution. He would appeal to Bellerophon's courage and propose a mission that would surely lead to the prince's death.

The next day Iobates summoned Bellerophon to his throne room. "I am very troubled," the king said. "My kingdom is being **devastated** by the Chimera, a fire-breathing monster with the head of a lion, the body of a goat, and the tail of a serpent. If only I could find someone brave enough to rid Lycia of this creature!" Just as Iobates had expected, the young prince proudly offered to attempt this dangerous deed.

Before undertaking his mission, Bellerophon consulted Polyidus, a wise **soothsayer**. "You will succeed in slaying the Chimera by riding on the winged horse Pegasus," predicted the soothsayer. "Go now to the temple of the goddess Athena, for she will help you."

That night Bellerophon fell asleep in a corner of the temple. He dreamed that Athena brought him a golden bridle. "Slip it over Pegasus's head," she told him. "Only then will you be able to mount this wild, swift horse." When the prince awoke, he was amazed to find the bridle lying by his feet. He rushed out to the fields and found Pegasus drinking at a spring. Soon, Bellerophon was soaring through the sky on the back of the beautiful winged horse.

When he spotted the Chimera, Bellerophon directed Pegasus to swoop down and circle over her head. The beast roared, lashed her scaly serpent's tail, and spewed scorching flames into the air. But the horse and rider were just above her reach. Bellerophon shot arrow after arrow into the monster's body. With a final fiery roar, the Chimera fell over and died.

King Iobates was stunned when the young prince returned and announced that he had killed the Chimera. He sent Bellerophon off on other **perilous** missions. But, with the help of Pegasus, he always came back in triumph. At last, the king decided that this bold hero was surely favored by the gods and shouldn't be killed. Instead, he honored Bellerophon with a great feast and gave him his daughter in marriage.

1. **Why did King Iobates feel that he was obliged to kill Bellerophon?**
   - ○ **A.** Bellerophon had offended his wife.
   - ○ **B.** He had been asked to do so by his son-in-law.
   - ○ **C.** Bellerophon had angered the gods.
   - ○ **D.** Bellerophon had forgotten to read the letter to him.

2. **In paragraph four, King Iobates tells Bellerophon that his kingdom is being <u>devastated</u> by the Chimera. Which of these is the best synonym for *devastated*?**
   - ○ **A.** watched
   - ○ **B.** entertained
   - ○ **C.** visited
   - ○ **D.** destroyed

3. **Bellerophon consulted Polyidus, a <u>soothsayer</u>. A *soothsayer* is someone who**
   - ○ **A.** can see into the future.
   - ○ **B.** teaches young men to tame and ride horses.
   - ○ **C.** sells weapons and armor to young heroes.
   - ○ **D.** is an expert on fire-breathing monsters.

4. **Where was Bellerophon when he had his dream?**
   - ○ **A.** in the sky, riding on Pegasus
   - ○ **B.** in the goddess Athena's temple
   - ○ **C.** at the spring where Pegasus was drinking
   - ○ **D.** in the palace of King Iobates

5. **According to the myth, why wasn't Bellerophon burned by the Chimera's flames?**
   - ○ **A.** He was protected by the golden bridle.
   - ○ **B.** He was wearing metal armor and heavy boots.
   - ○ **C.** He was circling far enough above the Chimera's head to avoid them.
   - ○ **D.** Pegasus covered him with his large wings.

6. **In the last paragraph, it says that King Iobates "sent Bellerophon off on other <u>perilous</u> missions." Which of these is the best antonym for *perilous*?**
   - ○ **A.** safe
   - ○ **B.** important
   - ○ **C.** brief
   - ○ **D.** interesting

7. **Which of the following statements about King Iobates is true?**
   - ○ **A.** He felt no respect for the gods and their wishes.
   - ○ **B.** He thought that Bellerophon would be killed by the Chimera.
   - ○ **C.** He was the king of Corinth.
   - ○ **D.** All of his children were sons.

8. **The title that best expresses the main idea of this myth is**
   - ○ **A.** The Taming of the Winged Horse Pegasus
   - ○ **B.** A Night in Athena's Temple
   - ○ **C.** A Sealed Letter From King Proetus
   - ○ **D.** The Triumphs of a Bold and Brave Hero

1. In our language, one meaning of the word *chimera* is "a horrible creature of the imagination." Let your imagination run wild and, in the boxes below, create a chimera. Be sure to give your creature a name.

Picture	Written Description

2. Do you think that Bellerophon knew what the sealed letter from King Proetus said? _____

   Why do you think this? _____

   _____

3. King Iobates was presented with a dilemma when King Proetus asked him to kill Bellerophon. What do you think a *dilemma* is? Take a good guess, then look it up in the dictionary to see if you're right.

   My guess: _____

   The dictionary definition in my own words: _____

   _____

4. What did Athena give to Bellerophon?

   _____

   What did it help him to do?

   _____

   _____

5. List the four adjectives that are used in the myth to describe Pegasus.

   _____

6. Why did Iobates think that Bellerophon was favored by the gods?

   _____

The Write Stuff

Do you sometimes remember your dreams? In your journal or on a separate sheet of paper, write about one of your dreams that was exciting, funny, weird, scary, or, like the dream that Bellerophon had, came true when you woke up.

Daedalus and Icarus

King Minos, the ruler of Crete, had a problem. To solve it, he needed the help of Daedalus, a very talented **architect** and inventor. Minos sent for Daedalus. "I want you to build something beneath my palace," said the king. "I need a maze with passages that twist and turn so much that no one can find a way out. I will call it my labyrinth."

When the labyrinth was finished, Minos was relieved. His problem was solved. He now had a place where he could safely keep the Minotaur, a horrible creature that was part bull and part man. The king put the Minotaur into his maze. Then, he forced seven young men and seven maidens to enter this dark, winding place. They were to be the food for this monster that only ate human flesh. The next year Minos sent 14 more victims into the maze.

After several years of this cruelty, a brave young man named Theseus volunteered to be enclosed in the labyrinth. The heroic youth killed the Minotaur, found his way out through the confusing tangles of the maze, and fled from Crete on a ship.

Minos was furious. He was sure that Daedalus must have helped Theseus escape from the labyrinth. Only its builder, the king reasoned, understood the plan of the maze. Minos called for his soldiers. "Lock Daedalus and his son Icarus in the palace tower," he shouted.

Poor Daedalus and Icarus! There was little to do but gaze out the window and feed the birds that flew into their room. But one day Daedalus exclaimed to his son, "I have an idea! We'll fly away, just as the birds do. You'll help me, Icarus. We'll make wings."

Day after day they plucked a few feathers from each bird that flew in to visit them. At last they had enough, and Daedalus set to work. He fashioned each wing by arranging feathers into three overlapping rows. Then, he joined the feathers together with small dabs of softened wax. When all four wings were finished, he bent each one so that it curved just like the wings of a bird. "Stay close to me," Daedalus advised his son. "And don't fly too high or the heat of the sun will melt the wax that's holding the feathers in place."

Daedalus and Icarus put on their wings, took off from the window ledge, and flew out over the sea. At first, Icarus carefully followed behind his father. But soon he became filled with the **exhilaration** of flying. He glided on currents of air. He swooped down toward the sea and then rose back up. Forgetting his father's warning, Icarus soared higher and higher. Boldly, he flew ever nearer to the blazing hot sun. Suddenly, the feathers of his wings began to come apart and flutter away. His father cried out to him. But there was nothing Daedalus could do but watch sadly as his son plunged into the sea, followed by a scattering of feathers.

1. **In the first line of this myth, it says that King Minos had a problem. What was that problem?**
   - ○ **A.** He didn't know what to do with the area underneath his palace.
   - ○ **B.** He didn't know how to get out of the labyrinth.
   - ○ **C.** He didn't have a safe place where he could keep the Minotaur.
   - ○ **D.** He didn't know what to feed the Minotaur.

2. **Daedalus was a highly skilled inventor and <u>architect</u>. An *architect* is someone who**
   - ○ **A.** studies the habits of birds.
   - ○ **B.** designs, draws plans for, and supervises the construction of buildings.
   - ○ **C.** teaches children.
   - ○ **D.** can see what will happen in the future.

3. **When he was younger, one of the characters in this myth killed Sciron, a fierce bandit who kicked travelers off of high rocks into the sea below. Based on what you know about them, who do you think carried out this courageous deed?**
   - ○ **A.** Theseus   ○ **B.** Icarus   ○ **C.** King Minos   ○ **D.** Daedalus

4. **Daedalus and his son had all of the following things in their room. Which did Daedalus use to fasten together the feathers?**
   - ○ **A.** water   ○ **B.** food   ○ **C.** spiders   ○ **D.** candles

5. **Based on what you read in this myth, you can conclude that King Minos's palace was**
   - ○ **A.** surrounded by high mountains.   ○ **B.** close to the sea.
   - ○ **C.** in a large city with many tall towers.   ○ **D.** near a dark, tangled forest.

6. **In the seventh paragraph, it says that Icarus "became filled with the <u>exhilaration</u> of flying." Which of these is the best synonym for *exhilaration*?**
   - ○ **A.** fear   ○ **B.** boredom   ○ **C.** exhaustion   ○ **D.** excitement

7. **All of these adjectives describe Icarus EXCEPT**
   - ○ **A.** foolish   ○ **B.** daring   ○ **C.** cautious   ○ **D.** helpful

8. **Some myths have a moral (a lesson to be learned from the story). Which of these is the best moral for this myth?**
   - ○ **A.** Only birds can fly.
   - ○ **B.** Helping a king with his problems can often lead to trouble.
   - ○ **C.** It is important to pay attention to advice from those who are older and wiser.
   - ○ **D.** It can be dangerous to go into a maze without knowing the way out.

1. On the pages of the instruction manual below, write simple, easy to follow directions for making wings like the ones that Daedalus made for himself and his son.

INSTRUCTION MANUAL
How to Make Wings

Step 1:	Step 2:	Step 3:	Step 4:
Gather a lot of feathers.			

2. What adjective do you think best describes King Minos?

   _____

3. Write a short description of the Minotaur.

   _____

4. Why did King Minos think that Daedalus must have helped Theseus find his way out of the maze?

   _____

   _____

5. Daedalus's escape plan was very ingenious. What do you think *ingenious* means? Take a good guess, then look it up in the dictionary to see if you're right.

   My guess: _____

   The dictionary definition in my own words: _____

   _____

6. List three verbs (action words) that are used in this myth to tell about how Icarus flew

   through the air. He _____ , _____ , and

   _____ .

The Write Stuff

Have you ever wished that you could fly? Fasten on some make-believe wings and soar into the sky. In your journal or on a separate sheet of paper, write about where you flew, what you saw, how it looked, and how you felt.

Demeter and Persephone

Demeter, goddess of the harvest, spent much of her time on earth, happily tending its fields and plants. She was often accompanied by her daughter, Persephone, who was as pretty as a rosebud and as gentle as a violet.

One day while they were visiting earth, Persephone wandered off to pick some flowers for her mother. Suddenly the ground split open near her feet. Out came a chariot pulled by snorting black horses and driven by Hades, god of the underworld and ruler of the dead. He snatched the terrified girl and carried her down through the earth to his lonely kingdom.

"Let me go!" cried Persephone angrily. "Return me to my mother!"

"Never," replied Hades. "You will be my queen and bring cheer to my gloomy palace."

Up on earth, Demeter had heard her daughter's desperate cries. She searched frantically for Persephone everywhere. But the ground had closed up, and no sign of the girl remained. Overcome with worry, Demeter called out to the god of the sun. "You see everything, Helios. Tell me what has become of my daughter."

"She was stolen by Hades to become queen of the underworld," answered Helios.

When she heard this, Demeter's heart filled with grief. She lost all interest in earth's fields and plants. Crops withered, trees dropped their leaves, and seeds no longer sprouted. In time, there was little to eat, and people began to starve. Zeus, the powerful king of the gods, begged Demeter to get back to her duties. "I will do nothing until my daughter is returned to me," the goddess declared.

Zeus realized that he had to take action. "I will send my son Hermes. He'll bring Persephone back to you, but only if she has eaten no foods of the underworld."

Persephone danced about joyously when she learned why Hermes had come to Hades' dark palace. Hades, on the other hand, was very upset. Hoping to prevent his pretty queen from leaving, he placed some juicy red pomegranate seeds in the palm of her hand. "You've been too sad to eat anything," he said. "Before you go, you must try this delicious fruit." Eager to go and ever so hungry, Persephone quickly ate a few of the sweet seeds.

Hermes wondered what he should do. He called upon Zeus to decide whether the girl had to remain in the underworld. "Persephone may return to her mother," Zeus ruled. "But each year she must spend time in Hades's palace—one month for each seed that she ate."

And that is why the earth becomes cold and **barren** every winter. Persephone is with Hades, and Demeter longs for her daughter. But every spring, when Persephone returns to her, Demeter is thankful. The earth becomes green and blossoms once again with flowers.

1. **Why did Hades want to take Persephone to the underworld?**
   - ○ **A.** He wanted her to be his queen.
   - ○ **B.** He was lonely in his kingdom.
   - ○ **C.** He thought she would bring cheer to his palace.
   - ○ **D.** all of the above

2. **Who told Demeter what had happened to her daughter?**
   - ○ **A.** Helios
   - ○ **B.** Hermes
   - ○ **C.** Zeus
   - ○ **D.** Hades

3. **Demeter stopped performing her duties because**
   - ○ **A.** she was bored with taking care of plants.
   - ○ **B.** Zeus gave her responsibilities to Hermes.
   - ○ **C.** she was too busy looking for Persephone.
   - ○ **D.** she was too sad to do anything.

4. **Zeus finally agreed to have Hermes bring Persephone back to her mother because**
   - ○ **A.** he longed to see Persephone again.
   - ○ **B.** he wanted to save the people on earth from starvation.
   - ○ **C.** he didn't like Hades and wanted to make him unhappy.
   - ○ **D.** he wanted Persephone to take over her mother's duties.

5. **According to the myth, why hadn't Persephone eaten any food while she was in the underworld?**
   - ○ **A.** There was nothing to eat in the underworld.
   - ○ **B.** She didn't like any of the foods that they had there.
   - ○ **C.** She had been too unhappy to eat anything.
   - ○ **D.** Hades wanted her to starve.

6. **In the last paragraph it says that every winter the earth becomes cold and barren. Which of these is the best antonym for *barren*?**
   - ○ **A.** fruitful
   - ○ **B.** dull
   - ○ **C.** slippery
   - ○ **D.** smooth

7. **Based on the ending of this myth, you can conclude that**
   - ○ **A.** Persephone ate 12 pomegranate seeds.
   - ○ **B.** Demeter returns to tending the fields and plants every spring.
   - ○ **C.** Persephone spends each summer and fall with Hades.
   - ○ **D.** Demeter and Hades did not agree to Zeus's ruling.

8. **As you read in this myth, the Greek name for the goddess of the harvest was Demeter. In ancient Rome, the name for the goddess of the harvest was Ceres. Which of these words in our language comes from the Roman name for this goddess?**
   - ○ **A.** certificate
   - ○ **B.** cereal
   - ○ **C.** circus
   - ○ **D.** certain

1. Adjectives and adverbs make sentences more interesting. Adjectives describe people, places, and things (nouns). Adverbs often describe action words (verbs). In the boxes below, list at least ten adjectives and five adverbs that are used in this myth.

DESCRIPTIVE WORDS

Adjectives	Adverbs
• •	•
• •	•
• •	•
• •	•
• •	•

2. To what two flowers is Persephone compared?

   _____

3. How did the god of the sun know what had happened to Persephone?

   _____

4. Do you think that Demeter was a good mother?

   _____

   Why or why not?

   _____

   _____

5. In this myth, Persephone was abducted by Hades. What do you think *abduct* means? Take a good guess, then look it up in the dictionary to see if you're right.

   My guess: _____

   The dictionary definition in my own words: _____

   _____

6. Why did Persephone have to return to the underworld each year?

   _____

   _____

The Write Stuff

Spring is a joyful season for Demeter because her daughter is with her again. What is your favorite season of the year? Write about it in your journal or on a separate sheet of paper.

Echo and Narcissus

Long ago there lived a pretty nymph named Echo. Almost never alone, she liked to play in waterfalls with the other nymphs and go hunting with the goddess Artemis. Echo was generous and warm-hearted, but she was also a chatterbox. Sadly, it was this love of talking that led to her harsh punishment by the goddess Queen Hera.

One day Hera was stalking through the woods, angrily searching for her husband Zeus, king of the gods. She had correctly suspected that he was once again on earth, flirting with some of the nymphs. Hoping to protect her friends from Hera's quick temper, Echo ran up to the goddess and began to talk on and on. By the time Hera was able to break away, the nymphs had fled and Zeus had returned to his home on Mount Olympus.

"You have deliberately delayed me with your **incessant** chatter!" Queen Hera shouted at Echo. "As punishment, you will never again speak except to repeat the last words of others."

Soon after that, poor Echo saw and fell in love with Narcissus, an extremely handsome youth who liked to spend his time alone, hunting for deer. Unable to speak to him of her love, Echo secretly followed him wherever he went. Finally, she gathered her courage. She stepped out from behind a tree and threw her arms around him. Narcissus, who felt no affection for anyone, pushed her aside. "Go away! I'd rather die than be with you," he said rudely. "Be with you," Echo tearfully replied. But Narcissus scornfully walked off into the woods.

Forlorn and ashamed, Echo hid in valleys and in caves. She slowly faded away until all that was left was her voice. It can still be heard today, softly answering those who call.

As for Narcissus, he was punished by the goddess Nemesis for his cruel treatment of Echo. "Narcissus, too, will feel the pain of unreturned love," the goddess declared. "I will make this cold-hearted youth who doesn't love others fall in love with himself."

On a warm afternoon, Narcissus stopped to rest by a clear, deep pool. As he bent down to drink from it, he saw the image of a handsome youth on the smooth surface of the water. Narcissus's heart filled with love. He stretched out his arms and tried to touch him. But each time he reached down into the water, the youth disappeared in a swirl of ripples.

Day after day Narcissus remained by the pool, gazing longingly at the image in the water. He couldn't tear himself away. Forgetting to eat, he became thinner and thinner until he finally faded away. It is said that a sweet-smelling flower with white petals sprang up in the place where he had sat for so long. This beautiful flower is called the narcissus.

1. **What is the main purpose of this myth's first paragraph?**
   - ○ **A.** to explain how Hera punished Echo
   - ○ **B.** to let readers know that Artemis, goddess of the hunt, was one of Echo's friends
   - ○ **C.** to introduce and describe Echo
   - ○ **D.** to explain that Echo lived long ago

2. **In the third paragraph, Hera says that Echo's <u>incessant</u> chatter has delayed her. Which of these is the best synonym for *incessant*?**
   - ○ **A.** loud
   - ○ **B.** wise
   - ○ **C.** endless
   - ○ **D.** guilty

3. **Hera punished Echo because**
   - ○ **A.** she was envious of Echo's lovely voice.
   - ○ **B.** Echo had kept her from catching Zeus with the nymphs.
   - ○ **C.** she had found Echo flirting with her husband.
   - ○ **D.** Echo hadn't talked about anything that was interesting.

4. **Based on what you read in this myth, you can conclude that Narcissus**
   - ○ **A.** had been in love many times.
   - ○ **B.** only liked talkative nymphs.
   - ○ **C.** liked to go hunting with his friends.
   - ○ **D.** didn't care if he hurt the feelings of others.

5. **In the fifth paragraph, it says that Echo felt <u>forlorn</u> and ashamed. Which of the following is the best antonym for *forlorn*?**
   - ○ **A.** cheerful
   - ○ **B.** frightened
   - ○ **C.** weak
   - ○ **D.** attractive

6. **Why didn't the youth that Narcissus saw in the pool come out to be with Narcissus?**
   - ○ **A.** He felt no affection for Narcissus.
   - ○ **B.** He preferred to stay in his watery home.
   - ○ **C.** He couldn't because he was Narcissus's reflection in the water.
   - ○ **D.** He wanted to punish Narcissus for his cruel treatment of Echo.

7. **Suppose Narcissus had said, "Pretty nymph, let's go hunting together." What would Echo have replied?**
   - ○ **A.** "I would love to go hunting with you."
   - ○ **B.** "Go hunting together."
   - ○ **C.** "Pretty nymph."
   - ○ **D.** "First tell me your name."

8. **This myth gives an explanation for why**
   - ○ **A.** the sound of the happy laughter of nymphs can still be heard at waterfalls.
   - ○ **B.** people like white flowers.
   - ○ **C.** ripples can be seen on the surface of deep pools.
   - ○ **D.** people can sometimes hear answers when they call out "hello" in places like caves.

1. Compare Echo and Narcissus in the Venn diagram below. In the center, list as many ways as you can in which these characters and what happened to them are alike. On the left and the right, list as many ways as you can in which these characters and what happened to them are different.

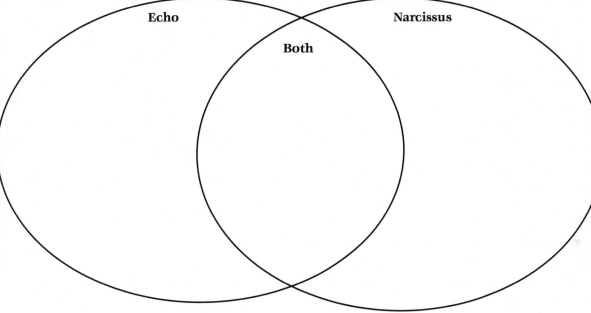

Echo   **Narcissus**

Both

2. Where was the home of the god Zeus?

   _____

   _____

3. Do you think that Echo deserved to be punished by Queen Hera? _____

   Why or why not?

   _____

   _____

4. The goddess Nemesis is often described as the goddess of vengeance. What do you think *vengeance* means? Take a good guess, then look it up in the dictionary to see if you're right.

   My guess: _____

   The dictionary definition in my own words: _____

   _____

The Write Stuff

Imagine that you are in the woods, sitting by a clear pool with a very smooth surface. You bend down and look into the pool. In your journal or on a separate sheet of paper, write in detail about what you see reflected in the water.

Io

Zeus, king of the gods, often flirted and fell in love with beautiful women. This made his wife, Queen Hera (at right), quite cross. She hated these rivals who took her husband's attention away from her.

One afternoon Zeus was on earth with Io, the beautiful young daughter of Inachus, a river god. Hera angrily rushed down to earth. Zeus, sensing her approach, changed Io into a snow-white cow. Hera pretended to be fooled. She praised the pretty cow and begged Zeus to give her the animal as a gift. Fearing her bad temper, Zeus reluctantly agreed.

Hera sent for her servant Argus. "Keep constant guard over my little cow," she instructed him. Argus was the perfect watchman. He had 100 eyes, and he never closed more than half of them when he slept.

Io felt quite upset and lonely. Abandoned by Zeus, she spent her days eating grass, always closely watched by Argus. One day, while she was grazing near a river, she saw her father. She tried to call out and tell him what had happened, but she could only moo and moo.

Zeus felt sorry for the suffering he had brought upon sweet Io, but he didn't dare help her himself. He called for his son Hermes and asked him to go to earth and find a way to set Io free. Hermes was a very cunning god. He dressed himself as a shepherd and walked up to Argus. "Let me play a tune for you on my shepherd's pipe," he said. Argus was glad for the company and listened happily to the soft music. After some time, Hermes began to tell him a very long and monotonous tale that went on and on and on. Argus became so bored that finally all of his eyes closed, and he fell fast asleep. Quickly, Hermes drew his sword and killed him.

Hera was **irate** when she saw that Argus was dead. To honor her loyal servant, she placed his 100 bright eyes on the tail of her favorite bird, the peacock. To this day the shiny (but unseeing) eyes of Argus can be seen on this bird's fancy tail feathers.

As for Io, she was now free, but remained a snow-white cow. Still angry, Hera sent a stinging gadfly to chase her. Io ran from land to land trying to escape the buzzing, biting insect. At last, Hera's heart softened. "Promise me that you will never look at Io again," she said to Zeus. He happily agreed. With that, he changed Io back into a beautiful young girl.

1. **The title that best expresses the main idea of this myth is**
   ○ **A.** The Stinging Gadfly
   ○ **B.** Hera's Punishment of Io
   ○ **C.** The Death of Argus
   ○ **D.** Hermes' Boring Story

2. **Why did Hera want Zeus to give her the snow-white cow?**
   ○ **A.** She thought it was pretty.
   ○ **B.** She wanted to use its milk to make cheese and butter.
   ○ **C.** She liked to collect animals and birds.
   ○ **D.** She wanted to make sure that Zeus would stop flirting with Io.

3. **Who was Io's father?**
   ○ **A.** Inachus   ○ **B.** Hermes   ○ **C.** Argus   ○ **D.** Zeus

4. **When Io saw her father, why didn't she call out and ask him for help?**
   ○ **A.** He was too far away.
   ○ **B.** She couldn't speak.
   ○ **C.** She was afraid that Argus would hurt her father.
   ○ **D.** She was too busy eating grass.

5. **How many of Argus's eyes were closed when Hermes killed him?**
   ○ **A.** 1,000   ○ **B.** 200   ○ **C.** 50   ○ **D.** 100

6. **In paragraph six it says, "Hera was <u>irate</u> when she saw that Argus was dead." Which of these is the best synonym for *irate*?**
   ○ **A.** angry   ○ **B.** embarrassed   ○ **C.** relieved   ○ **D.** puzzled

7. **What did Zeus do that was pleasing to Hera?**
   ○ **A.** He sent his son Hermes down to earth to set Io free.
   ○ **B.** He flirted with beautiful women.
   ○ **C.** He promised her that he would not look at Io any more.
   ○ **D.** He gave her a peacock with beautiful feathers.

8. **Based on what you read in this myth, you can conclude that Hera**
   ○ **A.** was very beautiful.
   ○ **B.** had many servants.
   ○ **C.** was a kind and gentle goddess.
   ○ **D.** was not easily tricked by Zeus

1. Fill in the chart with the name of the character that you think is best described by each adjective. Then write your reason for each of your choices. (Use each character only once.)

ADJECTIVE	CHARACTER	REASON WHY
clever		
regretful		
miserable		
jealous		

2. Why was Argus a good choice to be a guard over Io?

    _____

3. What instrument did Hermes play for Argus?

    _____

4. According to the myth, why do peacocks have shiny eyes on their tail feathers?

    _____

    _____

5. Why did Io run from land to land after Argus had been killed?

    _____

    _____

6. What adjective do you think best describes how Io felt at the end of this myth?

    _____

    Why?

    _____

    _____

The Write Stuff

You are about to be changed into an animal, but, unlike Io, you can pick the animal you'll be changed into. In your journal or on a separate sheet of paper, write about the animal you'd want to become, why you picked that animal, and what your life as that animal would be like.

Odysseus and Polyphemus

Odysseus, the king of Ithaca, sailed away from Troy with his men. He was eager to return home to his palace after winning a war. But storms and **turbulent** seas drove the ships far off course. After many days under sail, the fleet came to an island. Leaving the ships at anchor, Odysseus and 12 of his men went onto the island to search for supplies.

They soon came to a very large cave. Inside it they found piles of firewood, baskets of cheeses, pails of milk, and pens filled with lambs. "Let's wait here and see who lives in this place. Perhaps he will give us some of his food," said Odysseus.

As it grew dark, a Cyclops named Polyphemus returned to the cave. He was a fierce giant with one enormous eye in the middle of his forehead. Polyphemus drove his sheep into the cave and rolled a huge stone across the opening. Turning, he saw Odysseus and his men. He seized two of them and hurled them to the ground, killing them instantly. Then, smacking his lips hungrily, he ate them. When he was finished, he lay down and fell sound asleep.

The men huddled together in terror. "I would try to kill the Cyclops with my sword," whispered Odysseus, "but then we would be trapped here forever. Not even 20 oxen could drag that stone away from the entrance."

The next morning Polyphemus ate two more of the men, washing them down with large swallows of milk. He left the cave with his flock of sheep and rolled the stone back in place. "We're doomed!" cried the men. But Odysseus told them that he had come up with a plan.

That night, Odysseus offered him some of the wine that he had brought with him. Polyphemus gulped it down greedily and demanded more. He began to reel about drunkenly and finally crashed to the ground, fast asleep. "Now is our chance," Odysseus told his men. They took up a wooden beam that they had sharpened at one end and blinded the Cyclops by thrusting it into his eye. Polyphemus woke up, howling in pain. He stumbled about wildly, but he couldn't find the men.

When morning came, Polyphemus rolled away the stone to let his flock out to graze. He sat by the opening, ready to grab any man who tried to escape. But the men had tied the sheep together in groups of three and hidden themselves by clinging onto the bellies of the middle sheep. Polyphemus felt around as the animals went out, but all that he felt was thick wool.

Odysseus and his men ran to their ships and readied the fleet to sail away. "Farewell, Polyphemus," shouted Odysseus. "Know that it was I, Odysseus, who blinded you." Hearing this, Polyphemus staggered out of his cave. "Then know this, Odysseus," he shouted back angrily. "My father is Poseidon, god of the sea. And he will punish you."

1. **Odysseus sailed away from Troy, eager to**
   - ○ **A.** take part in a war.
   - ○ **B.** explore unknown lands with his men.
   - ○ **C.** find a fierce Cyclops named Polyphemus.
   - ○ **D.** return to Ithaca.

2. **In the first paragraph, it says that "storms and <u>turbulent</u> seas drove the ships far off course." Which of these is the best antonym for *turbulent*?**
   - ○ **A.** salty
   - ○ **B.** shallow
   - ○ **C.** calm
   - ○ **D.** dangerous

3. **Which of these did Odysseus and his men NOT find stored in the cave?**
   - ○ **A.** baskets of cheeses
   - ○ **B.** piles of firewood
   - ○ **C.** large quantities of wine
   - ○ **D.** pails of milk

4. **Why didn't Odysseus kill Polyphemus with his sword?**
   - ○ **A.** He was afraid to get too close to the Cyclops.
   - ○ **B.** He realized that only the Cyclops could roll back the stone.
   - ○ **C.** He had forgotten to bring his sword with him to the island.
   - ○ **D.** His sword wasn't strong enough to kill a giant.

5. **Which of these emotions best describes how the men felt when they cried, "We're doomed"?**
   - ○ **A.** hopeless
   - ○ **B.** energetic
   - ○ **C.** friendly
   - ○ **D.** bold

6. **Why did Odysseus offer wine to Polyphemus?**
   - ○ **A.** He wanted the Cyclops to owe him a favor.
   - ○ **B.** He had put poison in the wine.
   - ○ **C.** He wanted the Cyclops to fall into a deep sleep.
   - ○ **D.** He thought that the Cyclops would like a drink after his meal.

7. **Poseidon is mentioned in this myth because he is**
   - ○ **A.** Polyphemus's father.
   - ○ **B.** the king of Ithaca.
   - ○ **C.** god of the caves.
   - ○ **D.** Odysseus's father.

8. **Based on the ending of this myth, you can predict that**
   - ○ **A.** Polyphemus will regain his sight.
   - ○ **B.** Odysseus and his fleet will sail safely back to Troy.
   - ○ **C.** Polyphemus will lose all of his sheep.
   - ○ **D.** Odysseus and his fleet will face new dangers.

Comprehension Homework Packets © 2007 by Jan Meyer, Scholastic Teaching Resources

1. A story map is a helpful way to identify the key elements in a story. Fill in the spaces below with the key elements of this myth.

MAIN CHARACTERS

Name and briefly describe the two main characters.

1.

2.

SETTING

Where does the myth take place?

PROBLEM

What problem must be solved?

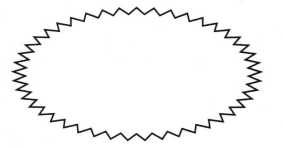

SOLUTION

List all of the steps that are taken to solve the problem.

2. Why did Odysseus and his men go onto the island? _____

_____

3. Why did Polyphemus roll back the stone on the morning that the men escaped?

_____

4. Do you think that Odysseus used good judgment when he shouted, "Know that it was I, Odysseus, who blinded you"?

_____

Why do you think this?

_____

_____

The Write Stuff

At the end of this myth, Polyphemus threatens Odysseus with punishment. In your journal or on a separate sheet of paper, write a tale of adventure in which Poseidon, the god of the sea, takes revenge on Odysseus.

Orpheus and Eurydice

There was no one on earth who made more beautiful music than Orpheus. His songs were so extraordinary that wild animals lay down quietly to listen, and trees pulled up their roots to follow him. It was no wonder he was so talented. His mother was Calliope, the Muse of poetry. She inspired him to create the lovely verses he sang. And it was the god Apollo who taught him to play his stringed instrument, called a lyre.

Orpheus loved a young woman named Eurydice. They married, but their happiness soon ended. A few days after their wedding, Eurydice stepped on a snake and died from its poisonous bite. The god Hermes gently led her soul down through the earth to the underworld.

Orpheus was heartbroken. Nothing cheered him, not even his music. "I will bring my wife back from the land of the dead," he vowed to his friends.

With his lyre in hand, Orpheus set out on his journey to the underworld. Near the sea, he entered a deep cave. Its dark, twisting passages led down and down through the earth. At last, Orpheus reached the banks of the Styx, the misty river that divides the land of the living from the shadowy underworld. He called out to the boatman Charon to row him across. "Only the dead may cross this river," the grim boatman declared. But when Orpheus played a sad melody on his lyre, Charon was so moved that he let him climb into his boat.

The iron gates to the land of the dead stood on the other side of the river. Guarding these gates was Cerberus, a fierce serpent-tailed dog with three ugly heads. Orpheus played his lyre again. Cerberus stopped snarling, lay down, and closed his six eyes. Orpheus passed quickly through the gates. Ahead of him was the palace of the god Hades, king of the dead.

Inside the **somber** palace, Orpheus found Hades seated on his black throne. Strumming softly on his lyre, he sang to Hades of his love for Eurydice and of his great loneliness. By the time his song was finished, the usually hardhearted king's cheeks were wet with tears. "Eurydice may return with you," Hades said. "But there is one condition. You may not turn around to look at her until you've reached earth's sunlight."

Orpheus set out for the upper world, followed silently by Eurydice. Was his wife really behind him or had he been tricked by Hades, he wondered anxiously. As he neared the mouth of the cave, he could no longer bear not knowing. Orpheus turned for one quick glance. There she was! But just as he joyously reached out for her, Eurydice faded back into the darkness with a whispered "Farewell."

1. **To make music with his lyre, Orpheus had to**
   - ○ **A.** press down on its keys.
   - ○ **B.** pluck its strings.
   - ○ **C.** shake it from side to side and make it rattle.
   - ○ **D.** hold it to his lips and blow into its mouthpiece.

2. **Orpheus and Eurydice were married for only a short time because**
   - ○ **A.** Eurydice decided to go off to live with Hades in his palace.
   - ○ **B.** Orpheus left Eurydice to go off to explore the underworld.
   - ○ **C.** Eurydice was grabbed and stolen away by the god Hermes.
   - ○ **D.** Eurydice died from a snakebite.

3. **Which of these words best describes how Orpheus felt when he decided to travel to the underworld to find his wife?**
   - ○ **A.** sorrowful
   - ○ **B.** shy
   - ○ **C.** curious
   - ○ **D.** tired

4. **Why didn't Charon want to row Orpheus across the River Styx?**
   - ○ **A.** His boat was already full of passengers.
   - ○ **B.** Only the dead were allowed to go across this river.
   - ○ **C.** He wanted to protect Orpheus from Cerberus who was on the other side of the river.
   - ○ **D.** Only gods were allowed to ride in his boat.

5. **How many eyes did the watchdog Cerberus have?**
   - ○ **A.** six
   - ○ **B.** two
   - ○ **C.** four
   - ○ **D.** eight

6. **In paragraph six, Hades's palace is described as <u>somber</u>. Which of these is the best synonym for *somber*?**
   - ○ **A.** colorful
   - ○ **B.** messy
   - ○ **C.** gloomy
   - ○ **D.** tiny

7. **Hades was in tears by the end of Orpheus's song because**
   - ○ **A.** he was a very kind and softhearted king.
   - ○ **B.** he knew he would miss Eurydice if she left his kingdom.
   - ○ **C.** he was deeply touched by Orpheus's very sad and beautiful song.
   - ○ **D.** he longed to be up on earth where it was sunny.

8. **Which of these feelings caused Orpheus to turn around to see if Eurydice was still behind him?**
   - ○ **A.** jealousy
   - ○ **B.** joy
   - ○ **C.** ambition
   - ○ **D.** doubt

1. In the box below, draw a picture map that shows the route that Orpheus followed on his journey to Hades's palace. Be sure to label everything with an identifying name.

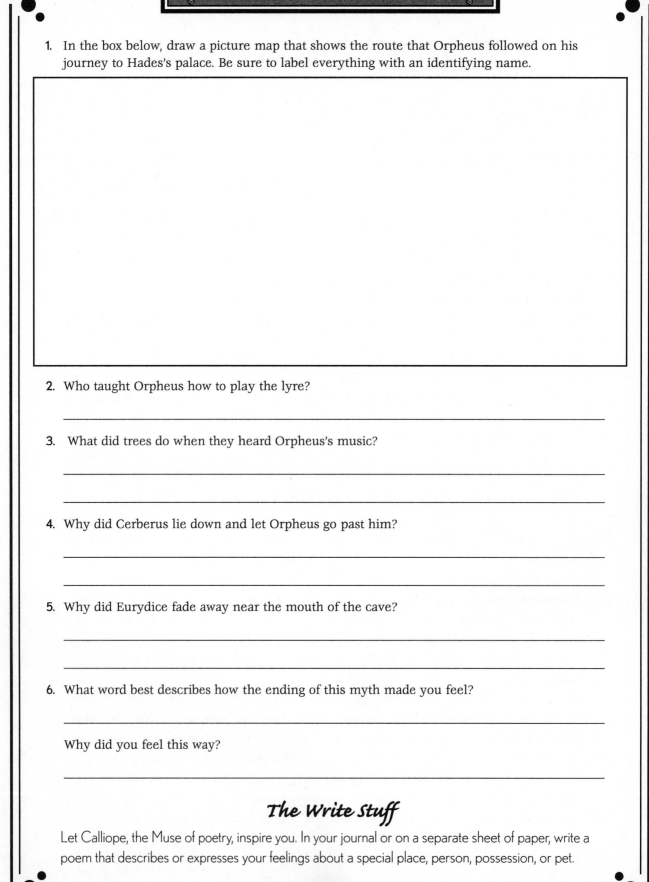

2. Who taught Orpheus how to play the lyre?

    _____

3. What did trees do when they heard Orpheus's music?

    _____

    _____

4. Why did Cerberus lie down and let Orpheus go past him?

    _____

    _____

5. Why did Eurydice fade away near the mouth of the cave?

    _____

    _____

6. What word best describes how the ending of this myth made you feel?

    _____

    Why did you feel this way?

    _____

The Write Stuff

Let Calliope, the Muse of poetry, inspire you. In your journal or on a separate sheet of paper, write a poem that describes or expresses your feelings about a special place, person, possession, or pet.

Perseus and Medusa

On the sunny island of Seriphus, a bold young man named Perseus lived with his mother, Danaë. The ruler of this island, King Polydectes, wanted to get rid of Perseus so that he could force the young man's mother to marry him. Being both **ruthless** and sly, the king soon came up with a deadly plan. He challenged Perseus to bring him the head of Medusa, a horrible Gorgon. This scaly, winged monster had a woman's face and a mass of hissing snakes for hair. She was so hideous and frightening that anyone who looked at her was turned to stone.

Perseus set out from Seriphus, wondering how he would ever accomplish his dangerous mission. Suddenly the goddess Athena appeared. "Take my shining shield and use it as a mirror when you attack Medusa. That way you won't have to look at her," she said.

Soon after that, Perseus turned and saw the god Hermes walking toward him. "I will lend you my strong sword," Hermes said. "Everything else that you need is with the nymphs of the North. But to find them, you must visit the Gray Women. Only they know the way to the nymphs' land, and it's a secret they carefully guard."

After many days of travel, Perseus reached the dim and **desolate** place where the three Gray Women lived. These wrinkled old women were sisters who shared a single eye and took turns looking through it. Perseus hid behind a rock and watched them pass the eye back and forth. At just the right moment, he jumped out and snatched the eye. "Gray Women," he shouted, "I have your eye. You won't get it back unless you tell me where to find the nymphs of the North." Desperate for their eye, the sisters quickly told him the way.

Journeying on, Perseus came at last to a beautiful and peaceful land behind the North Wind. It was here that the nymphs of the North lived. The nymphs greeted him warmly and gave him the three things he needed: a pair of winged sandals, a cap of darkness that would make him invisible, and a magic sack into which he could put Medusa's head.

Perseus tied on the sandals and flew to the island where Medusa dwelled. Down below, he saw stone statues of men scattered everywhere. Perseus shuddered and put on the cap of darkness. Remembering to look only at the reflections in Athena's shield, he found Medusa and hovered over her. With just one stroke, he cut off her horrifying head. He stuffed it, wriggling snakes and all, into his sack and flew away.

When Perseus returned to Seriphus, he learned that his mission had been a wicked scheme to get rid of him. Perseus went at once to Polydectes's throne room. As he pulled Medusa's head from the sack, he closed his eyes and shouted, "Here is the head you wanted!" The king looked at the head in amazement and was instantly turned to stone.

1. **Based on what you read in this myth, you can conclude that the kingdom that was ruled by King Polydectes was**

   ○ **A.** surrounded by water.   ○ **B.** always cold and gloomy.

   ○ **C.** behind the North Wind.   ○ **D.** being destroyed by Medusa.

2. **In the first paragraph, the king is described as "being both <u>ruthless</u> and sly." Which of these is the best antonym for *ruthless*?**

   ○ **A.** kind   ○ **B.** cruel   ○ **C.** smart   ○ **D.** handsome

3. **Which of these statements about Medusa is NOT true?**

   ○ **A.** She had wriggling snakes for hair.

   ○ **B.** After Perseus killed her, she lost the power to turn people to stone.

   ○ **C.** She had wings and the face of a woman.

   ○ **D.** She lived on an island.

4. **Based on what you read in this myth, you can conclude that King Polydectes**

   ○ **A.** didn't believe that Perseus's mother, Danaë, would willingly marry him.

   ○ **B.** was worried that Perseus would try to stop his marriage to Danaë.

   ○ **C.** hoped that Perseus would die while trying to kill Medusa.

   ○ **D.** all of the above

5. **Which of these did Perseus use to get the Gray Women to tell him where to find the nymphs of the North?**

   ○ **A.** flattery and charm   ○ **B.** coaxing and begging

   ○ **C.** fast thinking and quick hands   ○ **D.** money and gifts

6. **In paragraph four, it says that the place where the Gray Women lived was "dim and <u>desolate</u>." Which of these is the best synonym for *desolate*?**

   ○ **A.** crowded   ○ **B.** fancy   ○ **C.** lonely   ○ **D.** busy

7. **Which of these made it possible for Perseus to slay Medusa without having to look at her?**

   ○ **A.** the cap of darkness   ○ **B.** Athena's shield

   ○ **C.** the magic sack   ○ **D.** winged sandals

8. **The main purpose of this myth is to**

   ○ **A.** explain why King Polydectes challenged Perseus to bring him Medusa's head.

   ○ **B.** demonstrate that Athena and Hermes were often helpful and generous.

   ○ **C.** explain why Greece has so many stone statues.

   ○ **D.** tell how Perseus accomplished his difficult mission.

1. At the top of each of the boxes below, write the name of a character or a group of characters who helped Perseus. Be sure to put these characters in the order in which they met him. Then, below these names, write how they helped Perseus.

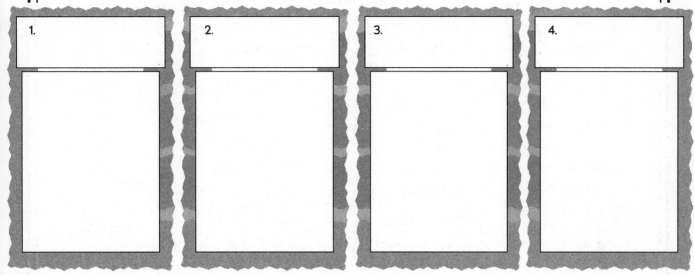

1.	2.	3.	4.

2. List at least three of the adjectives that are used to describe the Gorgon Medusa.

_____

3. What word do you think best describes how Perseus was feeling just before Athena appeared?

_____

Why do you think he was feeling that way?

_____

_____

4. Each of the three Gray Women had a small pit in the middle of her forehead. What do you think this pit was for?

_____

5. Describe the place where the nymphs of the North lived.

_____

6. What evidence is given in this myth that Perseus wasn't the first person who had been to the place where Medusa lived?

_____

_____

The Write Stuff

It's your turn to put on the cap of darkness and become invisible. In your journal or on a separate sheet of paper, write about where you would go and what you would do. Let your imagination run wild!

Phaeton

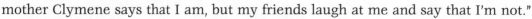

Young Phaeton entered the gleaming throne room of the palace of the sun. There, wearing a purple robe, sat Helios, the radiant god of the sun. His throne sparkled with glittering diamonds, and his crown blazed with dazzling, golden beams.

"I've traveled here, Helios, to find out if I am really your son," said the boy. "My mother Clymene says that I am, but my friends laugh at me and say that I'm not."

"Come here and let me **embrace** you, Phaeton," the sun god replied. "I am indeed your father. To prove it, you may ask me for anything and I'll give it to you. This I swear to by the Styx, the river of unbreakable oaths."

"Oh Father," the boy exclaimed, "I do have a wish. Every day you bring light to the world. I want, just once, to do as you do and drive the sun chariot across the sky."

Helios immediately regretted his promise. "Please ask for something else," he begged his son. "The trip is much too dangerous. The path is steep, the height to which you must climb is dizzying, and the fiery horses are too strong for you to control." But Phaeton insisted that this was his only wish and his greatest dream. At last, Helios had no choice but to give in.

The time to start the journey across the heavens was drawing near. The stars were beginning to fade, and the moon would soon disappear. Helios led the boy out to the place where the golden-wheeled chariot stood. Its horses were snorting, impatient to leave. "I fear for your safety," said the god as he set his crown on Phaeton's head. "Hold the reins tightly and spare the whip," he advised. "Stay on the path and drive neither too high nor too low."

Dawn threw open the gates of the east, and the horses swiftly sprang through them. As the glowing chariot rose up into the sky, Phaeton was filled with excitement and pride. But, before long, the fire-breathing horses sensed untrained hands on the reins. They left the well-worn path, causing the chariot to swing and tip wildly. Trembling with terror, Phaeton dropped the reins. The horses, now totally out of control, rushed up into the highest heavens and then plunged down close to the earth. Scorched with heat, the forests and fields caught fire. Seas shrank, and lakes dried up. Mother Earth cried out in pain to the gods for help.

Zeus, king of the gods, knew he had to act quickly if the earth was to be saved. Taking careful aim, he hurled a thunderbolt. The chariot broke apart, and Phaeton fell from the sky into the River Eridanus. Helios watched sadly as the water nymphs buried the boy who had set out so boldly to achieve his greatest dream.

1. **Phaeton's friends laughed at him because**
   - ○ **A.** he was too weak to drive the chariot of the sun.
   - ○ **B.** his father was a god.
   - ○ **C.** he looked silly wearing his father's crown of golden beams.
   - ○ **D.** he boasted that his father was the god of the sun.

2. **In the third paragraph, Helios asks his son to come to him so that he can embrace him. Which of these is the best synonym for *embrace*?**
   - ○ **A.** warn
   - ○ **B.** hug
   - ○ **C.** punish
   - ○ **D.** forgive

3. **Helios had to keep his promise to give his son anything he wanted because**
   - ○ **A.** he thought it would make Clymene happy.
   - ○ **B.** it was nearly time to drive the chariot of the sun across the sky.
   - ○ **C.** he had sworn to that promise on the Styx, the river of unbreakable oaths.
   - ○ **D.** he thought it would be an exciting experience for Phaeton.

4. **Based on what you read in this myth, you can conclude that the sun chariot's route across the sky was**
   - ○ **A.** east to west.
   - ○ **B.** north to south.
   - ○ **C.** west to east.
   - ○ **D.** south to north.

5. **What advice did Helios give to his son about driving the chariot?**
   - ○ **A.** to use the whip on the horses
   - ○ **B.** to stay close to the earth
   - ○ **C.** to grasp the reins firmly in his hands
   - ○ **D.** to drive neither too fast nor too slow

6. **Which of these adjectives best describes how Helios felt when Phaeton left to drive the chariot across the sky?**
   - ○ **A.** proud
   - ○ **B.** worried
   - ○ **C.** calm
   - ○ **D.** amused

7. **Why wasn't Phaeton able to control the sun chariot's horses?**
   - ○ **A.** The horses were untrained.
   - ○ **B.** The path was too worn.
   - ○ **C.** The horses were breathing fire from their mouths.
   - ○ **D.** Phaeton didn't have his father's strength or experience.

8. **As you read in this myth, the Greek name for the god of the sun was Helios. In ancient Rome, the name for the god of the sun was Sol. Which of these words in our language comes from the Roman name for this god?**
   - ○ **A.** solar
   - ○ **B.** solve
   - ○ **C.** solid
   - ○ **D.** soldier

1. Cause-and-effect relationships are often used in developing stories. They explain why actions and events happen and why decisions are made. In each row below, fill in the missing cause (reason why) or effect (what happened or resulted).

CAUSE	EFFECT
Helios told Phaeton that he could ask for anything he wanted.	
	The earth began to burn.
Mother Earth begged the gods to help her.	

2. List three of the synonyms for shining that are used in the first paragraph of this myth.

_____

3. What is one of the reasons that Helios thought driving his chariot would be too dangerous for Phaeton

_____

_____

4. How often did Helios drive his chariot across the sky?

_____

5. What do you think would have happened if Zeus had not thrown the thunderbolt?

_____

_____

6. What adjective do you think best describes Phaeton?

_____

Why did you pick this adjective?

_____

_____

The Write Stuff

Have you ever tried to do something that turned out to be harder than you had expected? Write about this experience in your journal or on a separate sheet of paper.

The Wooden Horse

Helen, the wife of King Menelaus of Sparta, was the most beautiful woman in the world. She and her husband lived happily together until a young prince named Paris carried her off. He took her to Troy, a rich and powerful city that was ruled by his father, King Priam.

Menelaus was enraged. He called upon the chieftains from all over Greece to help him get Helen back and take vengeance on her captor's city. Before long, a fleet of one thousand ships set sail for Troy. Each was filled with warriors eager to bring honor to Greece.

Troy, which lay near the coast, was surrounded by a high wall. For years the Greeks and Trojans fought fiercely outside this wall. Spears and arrows flew, swords clashed, and many **valiant** men died. The gods and goddesses even joined in the fight—some helping the Greeks, some helping the Trojans. But neither side could gain victory.

By the tenth year of the war, the Greeks were battle-weary and discouraged. They might have given up if Odysseus, their wisest warrior, had not come up with a cunning plan.

The next day the Greeks began constructing a huge, hollow wooden horse. When it was finished, a group of brave warriors climbed inside. Then, all but one of the remaining men sailed away and hid their ships on the far side of a nearby island. Left alone in their camp was Sinon. He had a very special role to play in Odysseus's plan.

The Trojans were amazed to see the Greek ships sail away. They streamed out of their city and ran to their enemy's abandoned camp. "They've given up!" they excitedly cheered. "Victory is ours!" But they were puzzled by the strange wooden horse that stood there.

Sinon then revealed himself. "The cruel Greeks turned against me and left me behind," he sobbed. He went on to tell the Trojans that the horse was an offering to the goddess Athena for a safe trip home. "They want you to destroy the horse and anger Athena," he explained. "Its large size is to discourage you from taking it into Troy and gaining Athena's favor."

Taken in by Sinon's story, the Trojans dragged the horse into their city and celebrated all day with singing, dancing, and feasting. When darkness fell, they wearily went home to sleep.

Later that night, Sinon helped the Greek warriors climb out of the horse. They ran to Troy's wall, overpowered the guards, and threw open the city gates. In poured the well-armed men from the ships that had returned to Troy. Taken by surprise, the Trojans were soon defeated. King Menelaus found beautiful Helen and joyously led her to his ship. As Troy burned down to ashes, he and the rest of the Greeks sailed home in triumph.

1. **King Menelaus wanted to take vengeance on the city of Troy because**
   - ○ **A.** it was a rich and powerful city.
   - ○ **B.** King Priam was his enemy.
   - ○ **C.** it was the city where Helen had been taken.
   - ○ **D.** he wanted to bring honor to Greece.

2. **All of the following weapons were used in the Trojan War EXCEPT**
   - ○ **A.** guns
   - ○ **B.** bows and arrows
   - ○ **C.** swords
   - ○ **D.** spears

3. **In paragraph three, it says, "many <u>valiant</u> men died." Which of these is the best synonym for *valiant*?**
   - ○ **A.** confused
   - ○ **B.** courageous
   - ○ **C.** clumsy
   - ○ **D.** cowardly

4. **Based on what you read in this myth, you can conclude that Troy was hard to conquer because**
   - ○ **A.** it had many strong warriors.
   - ○ **B.** it was protected by a high wall.
   - ○ **C.** it was helped in the war by some of the gods and goddesses.
   - ○ **D.** all of the above

5. **According to the myth, who was the wisest of the Greek warriors?**
   - ○ **A.** Odysseus
   - ○ **B.** Paris
   - ○ **C.** Sinon
   - ○ **D.** King Menelaus

6. **Sinon's very special role in Odysseus's plan was to**
   - ○ **A.** tell the Trojans a story about his cruel treatment by the Greeks.
   - ○ **B.** trick the Trojans into destroying the wooden horse.
   - ○ **C.** convince the Trojans that the Greeks had given up and sailed home.
   - ○ **D.** trick the Trojans into bringing the wooden horse into their city.

7. **The Greeks made the wooden horse very large because they wanted to**
   - ○ **A.** please the goddess Athena.
   - ○ **B.** prevent the Trojans from taking it into their city.
   - ○ **C.** be able to fit a group of soldiers inside its hollow body.
   - ○ **D.** frighten the Trojan soldiers.

8. **What quality was the most important in helping the Greeks finally conquer Troy?**
   - ○ **A.** strength
   - ○ **B.** cleverness
   - ○ **C.** caution
   - ○ **D.** anger

1. Newspapers use headlines to capture readers' attention. Make headline news out of some of the exciting events in this myth by completing the headlines below. Be sure to make your headlines short, clear, and eye-catching.

> **Queen Helen**
>
> **Greek Warriors**
>
> **Huge Wooden Horse**
>
> **Trojans**

2. Hector, the son of King Priam, was the leader of the Trojan army. What is the name of one of Hector's brothers?

   _____

3. The Trojans and the Greeks were adversaries. What do you think an *adversary* is? Take a good guess, then look it up in the dictionary to see if you're right.

   My guess: _____

   The dictionary definition in my own words: _____

   _____

4. Why was the Greek army discouraged in the tenth year of their war with Troy?

   _____

5. Where did the Greeks hide their ships when they pretended to sail home to Greece?

   _____

6. Give two reasons why you think it would be hard for the Greek warriors to stay crouched inside the wooden horse.

   _____

   _____

The Write Stuff

Do you have a nose for news? In your journal or on a separate sheet of paper, write a newspaper article about something interesting or exciting that's happened in your school or home. Be sure to include an attention-getting headline.

ANSWER KEY

Page 5
1. c 2. d 3. a 4. b 5. d 6. c 7. b 8. c

Page 6
1. Sample answers: 1585—The first colonists built houses and a fort. 1586—The colonists sailed back to England with Sir Francis Drake. 1587—Elizabeth Dare gave birth to a daughter. 1590—John White found that the settlement had been abandoned.
2. They reported that the peas they had planted had grown 14 inches in ten days.
3. He thought they would be more likely to make the colony a permanent settlement.
4. There was a war between England and Spain.
5. Sample answer: sad—He was leaving his daughter and new granddaughter.
6. speculate: to make guesses or to wonder and think about a specific subject

Page 8
1. b 2. c 3. c 4. b 5. d 6. a 7. d 8. c

Page 9
1. Sample answers for Ben Franklin: Date of birth—January 17, 1706; Free-time interests and activities—reading, fishing, rowing, swimming; Descriptive adjective—clever; he invented an interesting way to swim without having to use any effort.
2. They needed candles because they didn't have electric lights.
3. It says that Benjamin was his father's fifteenth child.
4. He read lots of books on a large variety of subjects.
5. Answers will vary.
6. He persuaded the French to help the colonies fight against the British.

Page 11
1. b 2. a 3. c 4. d 5. d 6. c 7. b 8. a

Page 12
1. Answers will vary.
2. "Taxation without representation" means that decisions about taxing the colonists were made without anyone from the colonies participating in the decisions.
3. The Parliament wanted to help the British East India Company.
4. Sample answer: They hid their identities because they knew that if the British knew they had participated they would get in trouble.
5. three ships
6. intolerable: unbearable or hard to endure

Page 14
1. b 2. c 3. a 4. d 5. d 6. c 7. b 8. d

Page 15
1. Sample answers: artistic—He made beautiful silver jewelry; determined—He worked year after year on his writing system and didn't give up; admired—He was honored with a medal by the Cherokee National Council.
2. They were taking land away from the Cherokee people.
3. Sequoyah was not paying attention to his family responsibilities.
4. There would be too many symbols for people to learn and remember.
5. Answers will vary. (Be sure that repeated syllables have the same symbols.)
6. literate: able to read and write

Page 17
1. c 2. c 3. d 4. d 5. b 6. a 7. a 8. c

Page 18
1. Sample answers: Council Bluffs—held their first official meeting with Native Americans; the Great Plains—saw huge buffalo herds; Fort Mandan—built a camp for the winter; Great Falls of the Missouri—carried their canoes and supplies around the falls; Camp Fortunate—Sacagawea found her long-lost brother; Columbia River—were greeted by the Wanapam Indians.
2. He hoped they would find a continuous water route to the Pacific Ocean.
3. Sample answers: food, clothing, medicines, journals, tents, guns, blankets, a compass, gifts for the Native Americans
4. The "great father" was President Thomas Jefferson.
5. a prairie dog
6. Sample answers: unfriendly Native American tribes, poisonous snakes, grizzly bears, biting mosquitoes, steep mountain passages, dangerous rapids, strong river currents

Page 20
1. c 2. d 3. b 4. c 5. a 6. b 7. c 8. d

Page 21
1. Cause—Isabella was sold to a new owner. Cause—Isabella was very angry because John Dumont had broken his promise to free her. Effect—She traveled around the country, speaking out against slavery.
2. New York
3. spirited, stirring
4. She also spoke about women's rights.
5. Sample answer: She was an inspiring speaker and faced her audiences with courage.
6. Sample answers: They had to find homes. They had to find jobs. Many could not read or write.

Page 23
1. c 2. c 3. d 4. c 5. b 6. b 7. a 8. d

Page 24
1. Answers will vary.
2. 36 rooms
3. a piano
4. They took place in Canada, at sea, and in the area of the Great Lakes.
5. Sample answer: worried—She was afraid that the British soldiers would attack Washington, D.C., and the White House.
6. pilfer: to steal small things

Page 26
1. d 2. b 3. c 4. c 5. b 6. d 7. a 8. c

Page 27
1. 1826—Moved to Battenville, New York; 1849—Began to work for the antislavery and temperance movements; 1853—Began to work for the women's rights movement; 1868—Began the newspaper called *The Revolution*; 1869—Founded the National Woman Suffrage Association with Elizabeth Stanton; 1872—Was arrested and found guilty of voting; 1906—Gave her last public speech; Died at the age of 86.
2. Sample answers: The girls had to sit in the back. The teacher didn't think that girls had to learn such things as long division.
3. She felt that if women were able to vote, they would be able to have an influence on social and political issues.
4. Elizabeth Cady Stanton
5. Sample answer: They thought that allowing women to vote was a ridiculous idea.
6. Sample answer: determined—She worked tirelessly for much of her life, trying to gain suffrage for women.

Page 29
1. d 2. c 3. b 4. b 5. a 6. b 7. a 8. c

Page 30
1. Women—governess, maid, dressmaker, nurse, hired family cook, laundress; Men—lawyer, banker, newspaper publisher, dentist, carriage driver, judge, factory owner, police officer, senator, butcher; Both—factory worker, school teacher, shop clerk, bakery worker
2. Sample answer: They felt that women were too sensitive, too delicate, and not smart enough to be doctors.
3. Sample answer: She did something that no other woman had ever done before.
4. They lived in crowded, unsanitary conditions.

Page 32
1. c 2. d 3. d 4. c 5. b 6. b 7. a 8. d

Page 33
1. Sample answers: Passeng[ers] traveled at night, risked bei[ng caught] by slave catchers; Conducto[rs—] both whites and African Am[ericans,] the most dangerous job; Stat[ions—] acted in secrecy, used signals to identify their stations
2. Tice Davids vanished from sight on the other side of the river, and his owner couldn't find him anywhere.
3. Answers will vary.
4. Answers will vary.
5. She was very successful in helping slaves escape from their masters.
6. He was known as the "President" of the Underground Railroad because he had sheltered a very large number of escaping slaves.

Page 35
1. c 2. b 3. a 4. d 5. b 6. b 7. c 8. d

Page 36
1. Sample answers (states should be in this order): Missouri—He developed a talent for caring for plants. Kansas—He attended high school. Iowa—He studied science and agriculture at Iowa State College. Alabama—He was the head of the department of agriculture at Tuskegee Institute.
2. He wanted to learn more than the one-room school in Neosho could teach him.
3. Sample answers: He taught classes. He directed crop and soil experiments. He gave advice about agriculture to farmers in outlying areas.
5. deplete: to empty or use up
6. It created a bigger market for peanuts. This helped farmers sell more of their peanut crops.

Page 38
1. b 2. b 3. d 4. d 5. c 6. a 7. b 8. c

Page 39
1. Sample answers: caring—Nurses took loving care of wounded and dying soldiers; brave—Jennie Hodgers faced enemy fire in more than 35 battles; clever—Sarah Edmonds used disguises to help her spy on the Confederate army.
2. delicate and dependent
3. They knit socks, made uniforms, and packed up donations of food and medicines.
4. Sample answer: Many people at this time felt that women belonged at home with their families. They also believed that women were not strong enough or courageous enough to take part in battles.
5. to be near their husbands, for excitement and adventure
6. espionage: the use of spies to gain secret information

Page 41
1. a 2. b 3. a 4. d 5. c 6. c 7. b 8. c

Page 42
1. Illustrations will vary but should be appropriate for each of the books, based on information given in the mini-biography or from the student's knowledge of the book.
2. Sample answers: I would not be able to play computer games. I would not be able to watch television.
3. She made her black, cashmere wedding dress.
4. She wanted to keep alive her memories of what it had been like to be a pioneer.
5. Isabel
6. The books have been translated into a number of languages.

Page 44
1. b 2. b 3. c 4. c 5. b 6. a 7. b 8. d

Page 45
1. Sample answers: Central Pacific—built eastward, had thousands of Chinese workers, laid track through the Sierra Nevada Mountains, laid track through the Nevada desert, used explosives to blast tunnels, threatened by avalanches, threatened by blasting powder accidents, faced heavy snows and winter storms, laid 690 miles of track. Union Pacific— built westward, had thousands of form[er] soldiers, many workers were Irish immigrants, laid track across the Grea[t] Plains, slept in boxcars, faced attacks b[y] Plains Indians, laid 1,086 miles of trac[k]. Both—had surveyors, had graders, had workers who laid down track, had trouble finding laborers, faced shortage[s] of materials, suffered from harsh weather, met at Promontory Point, workers were tough and brave.
2. Sample answers: by stagecoach, by horseback, by wagon, by walking, by ship around South America
3. The surveyors mapped the best rou[te] for the railroad tracks.
4. Sample answer: Their work was ver[y] hard and sometimes very dangerous.

Page 47
1. b 2. d 3. d 4. b 5. c 6. a 7. d 8. c

Page 48
1. Who—Wilbur and Orville Wright; When—December 17, 1903; Where—Ki[ll] Devil Hills, near Kitty Hawk, North Carolina; What—The Wright Brothers became the first to pilot and control a powered aircraft. Why—It led to the further development of airplanes and t[o] advances in aviation.
2. Wilbur was older.
3. finding a way to control the airplane during flight
4. They had succeeded in piloting controlled glides with their gliders.
5. It had two propellers, cloth-covered wings, a lightweight gasoline engine, an[d] controls similar to those in their 1902 glider.
6. Sample answer: nervous—He didn't know whether he would succeed in flying the plane or end up injuring himself.

Page 50
1. c 2. b 3. d 4. a 5. b 6. b 7. d 8. c

Page 51
1. 1920—Women won the right to vote. 1929—The Great Depression started. 1941—The U.S. entered World War II. 1945—The United Nations was established. World War II ended.
2. She lived with her grandmother because both her mother and her father had died.
3. Sample answers: the fight to end chil[d] labor, the fight to improve working conditions for women
4. the United Nations
5. Sample answers: courageous, caring, energetic, involved, important, hard-working, influential, intelligent
6. humanitarian: someone who cares about the well-being of human beings

Page 53
1. a 2. d 3. c 4. b 5. c 6. b 7. d 8. c

Page 54
1. Sample answers: 1865—Laboulaye suggested creating the statue. 1871—Bartholdi went to the United States to ge[t] support for the idea. 1875—France began raising funds for the statue. 1881—Hunt was selected to design the pedestal. 1884—Construction of the statue was completed. 1885—Statue was shipped to the United States. 1886—Dedication ceremony for the statue took place.
2. They talked about how France had helped the American colonies in the Revolutionary War.
3. It stood in a courtyard outside Bartholdi's workshop.
4. gigantic, huge, enormous
5. Bedloe's Island
6. the signing of the Declaration of Independence

Page 56
1. c 2. d 3. b 4. b 5. a 6. d 7. c 8. d

Page 57
1. Sample answers: 1916—Ruth Pitches 13 Scoreless Innings; 1920—Babe Ruth Sold to Yankees or Ruth Slams 54th Home Run; 1935—Ruth Sets Record with 714th Home Run
2. rundown